Inspirational Poems
of Encouragement

Inspirational Poems of Encouragement

Cover design by Kent Grey-Hesselbein,

KGB Design Studio

Manchester, TN, USA

http://kghdesign.nvaazion.com/

Inspirational Poems of Encouragement

by

Philip C. Vinson

Original file prepared by

Shirley Prather

Final manuscript

prepared and edited by

Stan St. Clair

Inspirational Poems of Encouragement

© 2010 by Philip C. Vinson,

St. Clair Publications

These individual poems may be copied and distributed freely to bless others so long as credit is given to Philip C. Vinson as the author. No one may in any way claim any of the verses contained herein as their own. Please contact St. Clair publications for further information, or to receive permission to include any poem or poems in any printed material.

ISBN 978-0-9826302-9-7

Printed in the United States of America by

St. Clair Publications

P. O. Box 726

Mc Minnville, TN 37111-0726

http://stan.stclair.net

Inspirational Poems of Encouragement

In loving memory of

Helen Le Compte Vinson

12-17-1932 to 3-18-2009

Inspirational Poems of Encouragement

Author's Introduction

Let me tell you a little about how I got started writing poetry.

It all started in February of '99 the week I became 68 years old. My wife, Helen, seemed down a little, and said sing to her. (You wouldn't want to hear me sing.) But when I began to talk, the words I spoke would rhyme.

After about six months, the type of poems changed. Many of the poems, at first, were for family.

Then I started writing poems like "God, Where Are You?", "Silent", "You Just Don't Care", "Heaven of Brass", and "You Did Not Come". I even wondered if He even wanted me to write some of them. But it seemed He did.

Then, on Christian T.V., I began to hear the very things I had written. I don't even know how many titles or something in one of my poems that I heard.

I believe they are for people that have gone through, or that are going through difficult times, pain, sorrow, or hurts that are depressed and discouraged. People who were praying or thinking those things that I wrote.

I believe they are to let people know that God loves them, He cares, and that He will never forsake them. He is closer than a brother. He is always near, even when it seems He is so far away.

Philip C. Vinson

Inspirational Poems of Encouragement

FORWARD

Isaiah 43:19 "Behold I do a new thing."

My beginning ii writing inspirational poetry came about unexpectedly in what has become a dear memory for my dear wife, Helen, and me. One day in late February, 1999, she asked me to sing to her. Usually this would be comforting, but as I sang, for the first time in my life, words came out that rhymed. Until then, at age 68, poetry had no interest to me. These words were forgotten, brought to a good laugh, and yet contained what my wife needed to hear.

My first poems were about four lines, and at times extended longer. A few were "Noah', "Wisdom", "Faith", "Satan", and "Family". Later came "God, Where Are You?" a sentiment experienced by many across our land.

Editor's note: Satan is not capitalized on purpose, except at the beginning of a line. This is to illustrate his smallness in comparison to God.

Inspirational Poems of Encouragement

TABLE OF CONTENTS

GOD, WHERE ARE YOU? 17

I MADE IT 18

SO HAVE I 19

THE TASK 20

YOU ARE THE CAUSE 21

MY NEW BIRTH 22

A FRIEND... 23

ADAM AND JESUS 24

NEVER ENDING STORMS 25

JOY 26

HOLY SPIRIT 27

A PURPOSE 28

BY IT 29

HE ALWAYS KNEW... 30

I KNOW 31

WHY? 32

LOVE 33

GRACE 34

THE GOOD NEWS 35

I'M JUST NOT SURE 36

Inspirational Poems of Encouragement

NEW BEGINNINGS……………………………………………… 37

PEARL OF GREAT PRICE ……………………………………… 38

COMING BACK ………………………………………………… 39

THAT OLD TREE …………………………………………….. 40

LORD I GIVE YOU PRAISE ...…………………………………. 41

TROUBLES EVERYWHERE ...……………………………….. 42

WEARY TO THE BONE ……………………………………….. 43

MY DILEMMA …………………………………………………. 44

DESPERATE CALL ……………………………………………. 45

TOMORROW ………………………………………………….. 46

JESUS …………………………………………………………… 47

THE WAY IT HAD TO BE ……………………………………… 48

WHEN , LORD?………………………………………………… 49

NEVER TOO OLD ……... ……………………………………... 50

BROKEN SPIRIT ………………………………………………... 51

IS LIFE WORTH LIVING? ……………………………………... 52

AMERICA ……………………………………………………… 53

DECISION ………………………………………………………. 54

WISDOM ……………………………………………………….. 55

WHAT AM I HERE FOR? ...…………………………………… 56

PROMISES ……………………………………………………. 57

YOUR LAST DAY………………………………………………. 58

Inspirational Poems of Encouragement

LORD GOD ALMIGHTY	59
WHAT IF HE HAD SAID NO?	60
HOLD ON TO YOUR FAITH	61
SURVIVING LIFE'S STORMS	62
SILENT	63
BEING LIKE THIS	64
INDEPENDENCE DAY	65
SIN	66
SOMEONE ALONG THE WAY	67
ONE DAY	68
NO OTHER TIME LIKE THIS	69
WHAT HAPPENS NEXT?	70
EVER SINCE	71
FROM THE PORTALS OF HEAVEN	72
YOU AND ME	73
I DID NOT QUIT	74
TIME OUT – PRAY	75
IT JUST WAITS ON GOD	76
THE TONGUE	77
WHEN I NEED YOU	78
A PRAYER FOR THE HURTING	79
THROW IN THE TOWEL	80

Inspirational Poems of Encouragement

YOU CHANGED MY LIFE 81

WHEN I GET OLD 82

I CAN ONLY IMAGINE 83

HEAVEN OF BRASS 84

IN CONTROL 85

THE CROSS 86

WILDEST DREAM 87

HEAVEN 88

IN HIM WE NOW ABIDE................................ 89

MORE LIKE THEE 90

GOD'S WORD SAYS 91

IN THE HOLLOW OF MY HAND 92

GOD'S MERCY 93

THIS PAIN 94

I REMEMBER 95

WHEN GOD TAKES A LOOK........................... 96

ON THE ROAD TO HELL 97

A CONVERSATION IN HEAVEN 98

ALL ALONE... 99

HAVE YOU FORGOTTEN ME 100

DRINK FROM HIS FOUNTAIN 101

YOU JUST DON'T CARE 102

Inspirational Poems of Encouragement

NEED A TOUCH 103

SERVANT 104

THAT BRIGHT AND MORNING STAR 105

THE SACRIFICE 106

DO WHAT'S RIGHT 107

REPENT 108

HE HAS RISEN 109

HIS COMING 110

NEVER PASS AWAY 111

MASTER PLAN 112

CAN THIS REALLY BE TRUE 113

I CAME 114

WHAT MORE COULD HE DO 115

YOU ARE GONE 116

SO DARK AND BLEAK 117

SHATTERED HOPES 118

BY FAITH... 119

THE ROCK 120

WHERE DID YOUR LOVE GO 121

SO MANY TIMES 122

YOU HEARD 123

THE STROKE 124

Inspirational Poems of Encouragement

I SHALL NOT WANT 125

THE BEACON 126

ALMOST TOO LATE 127

I NEED TO KNOW 128

WOULD MEAN SO MUCH 129

MY PAST 130

I AM 131

ON JUDGMENT DAY 132

SINS OF AMERICA 133

I WISH 134

GOD YET MAN 135

A REASON 156

LOST 137

DON'T WORRY 138

KING OF GLORY 139

DO IT GOD'S WAY 140

I BELIEVE 141

SOME OTHER TIME LORD 142

WAIT ON YOU 143

THE GRAVE 144

IT WAS ENOUGH 145

WHEN FIRST WE DID MEET 146

Inspirational Poems of Encouragement

TRUE TO MINE 147

IF THERE WAS NO FORGIVENESS? 148

ALL THIS HELL 149

ECHOES OF TIME 150

WHEN HE COMES I WILL GO...151

PATIENCE WEARING THIN 152

PICKING ON ME 153

TANGLED IN SATAN'S WEB..154

WITH YOU THE ANSWER STAYED 155

YOU WILL WIN 156

YOU ASK NO LESS 157

A LITTLE TASTE OF HEAVEN 158

CAUGHT UP..159

WEARINESS.. 160

NOW IT IS TOO LATE... 161

EVERYTHING IS GOING WRONG..................................... 162

HE IS FAITHFUL AND JUST...163

WHEN WILL YOU VISIT ME?...164

COMPLAIN...165

THOUGHTS..166

NINE-ONE-ONE...167

THE RIGHT ONE...168

Inspirational Poems of Encouragement

WHY OTHERS, NEVER ME? 169

THINGS..170

I DIDN'T KNOW………………………………………………171

IF..172

APPEAR IN GOD'S COURT……………………………………173

HIS NAME ……………………………………………………..174

YOUR DAY BEFORE GOD …………………………………… 175

SEEK ME ……………………………………………………… 176

I AM SAFE …………………………………………………….. 177

LOST HER WAY ……………………………………………… 178

WHY DID I LET THIS BE? ……………………………………. 179

I WANT TO SHARE……………………………………...….… 180

OUR TROOPS, OUR VETERANS ……………………………… 181

THE EARLY YEARS……………………………………………182

THE LATTER YEARS………………………………………… 183

YOU DID NOT COME…………………………………………184

JESUS LORD OF ALL`…………………………………………185

IN YOUR WORD I DELIGHT ……………………………...…. 186

MAKE MY HEART PURE …………………………....……….187

Inspirational Poems of Encouragement

Inspirational Poems of Encouragement

GOD, WHERE ARE YOU?

It's been a long time since Your glory has been shown,
Why must I face these mountains alone?
All these battles seem to abound,
Where are You, where is Your outstretched hand?

Where were You, God, when I was in need?
Why did You not come at my plead?
When I called, why did you not heed?
Where were You when I was in need?

At times do you feel alone?
God, where are You, are You never home?
Are You always on the go?
Do you have to continue to hunt, is it so?

God, are You really so far away,
That You can't hear me when I pray?
Don't you see all these things keep piling up?
Won't you come and empty this cup?

Now God, before I complain too much,
Just realize I am but human and need a touch,
A touch from that precious hand;
That hand that suffered wrong in our land.

God, this dry spell seemed so long,
I didn't feel like singing a song.
But You did come just in time,
And gave me little phrases that would rhyme.

Now thank You that this season is finished,
And my dry soul is replenished.
You were not early but You were never late,
To keep your appointment, to keep your date.

Now God, I realize You were never far away.
You were there for me every day.
Lord, forgive me for the way I felt,
Now let my heart before You melt.

Inspirational Poems of Encouragement

I MADE IT

I did not know what lay ahead for me today,
But God guided me each step of the way.
I made up my mind to fight, and not just sit…
I made it.

If I need help to make it, though heavy may be the cross,
I will have the help I need; I will never be at a loss.
Being a loser I am not, I did not quit…
I made it.

When my temptations come, and I am tried,
God was there, His face from me He did not hide.
In this day of need, my life to You I submit…
I made it.

If the river I crossed seems so wide,
Jesus says I will be there by your side.
He gave me the strength and the grit…
I made it.

The battle was on every side, the way seemed barred,
I have a reputation to uphold, it must not be marred.
The battle I won, I escaped the snares and the pit…
I made it.

The storm is raging without and within,
Will I make it, is my endurance wearing thin?
I have not come this far just to quit.
I made it.

You also might have to face life's stormy sea,
Christ says, "Be not afraid, with you I will always be".
You can overcome this power from God you get…
You made it.

If I live until the rapture takes place,
Each day I was kept by His grace.
So when by His resurrection power I am hit,
Then I can truly say I made it.

Inspirational Poems of Encouragement

SO HAVE I

Life has sure been a rocky road,
And each day heavier becomes the load.
Have you wished your troubles would pass you by?
Well, so have I.

Every mountain top will not have the answer for you.
It might not reveal what God wants you to do.
Or the valley might not reveal His will for the day.
But press on; He will meet you along the way.

This cross, Lord, is sure taking its toll.
By Your grace I will reach my goal.
I was hoping soon to hear from You.
Lord, won't You hear my prayer, too?

Life's storms come and you think you can't go on,
Lift your voice and make up your own song.
Jesus will be listening with an open ear.
Your song will be beautiful and He will hear.

Do your prayers seem to go unheard?
You have always prayed, and kept His Word.
But now you are not sure which way to go.
Lord, won't You come today and let me know?

Lord, I pray I hear when You speak.
And Your will I always seek.
Even if I do complain, it is still You I long for.
And Your Holy Name I do not want to mar.

Go ahead with your song of praise.
And before Him your voice in thanksgiving raise.
Because to you salvation Christ brought.
And He was never as far away as you thought.

Inspirational Poems of Encouragement

THE TASK

The task ahead is very great,
My Word must reach the people, or it will be too late.
So everyone must be prepared to tackle the task.
I will give you power to do what I ask.

I will not ask you to do this task alone,
Through you I will make My power known.
There will be battles you have not faced before,
But I will give you grace, and more.

Father, in Your work I want to be a part,
To encourage others to find a new start.
Thank You, Lord, for Your task You have given me,
I want to be for you all I can be.

I am not worried about what lies ahead for me.
I know with me You will always be.
You say there is much yet to do,
I want to work, until with me you are through.

Even as I do what You ask,
To get these words to the hurting is a big task.
But if I give then to a friend and give them out,
I believe that is what this is all about.

Do not worry about what you will face ahead,
I give you power to do what I want done and said.
Remember people are dying every day,
My children sleep, they need to fast and pray.

Just as I came to do what My Father did ask,
For you, I did not consider it too much of a task.
With Me, the task will not be too great,
And the job will get done before it is too late.

Inspirational Poems of Encouragement

YOU ARE THE CAUSE

Life first began with God's breath.
Now it begins with His death.
We were kept from a life of bliss.
Adam, you are the cause of this.

We were never meant to grow old and die.
But live forever and worship God Most High.
The way life was meant to be we now miss.
Adam, you are the cause of this.

Judas was chosen; with Christ he walked.
And with Him he talked.
Then he betrayed our Lord with a kiss.
Adam, you are the cause of this.

God meant for life to be a pleasure.
Adam, you kept us from this treasure.
I wonder if at our Lord they did hiss.
Adam, you are the cause of this.

Life could have been filled with joy and peace
And life that would never cease.
Because of what you did, Heaven many will miss.
Adam, you are the cause of this.

Since then so many have lost their way;
Christ had to pay for what you did that day.
All could have enjoyed earthly bliss.
Adam, you are the cause of this.

God saw the sinful state man was in.
He would have to suffer and die because of sin.
But Heaven we no longer have to miss.
Christ's death: Adam, you are the cause of this.

Inspirational Poems of Encouragement

MY NEW BIRTH

I am sorry, for all You had to go through for me.
But if You hadn't, in hell I am sure I would be.
Your love for me was so great.
It took Your death to remove my guilt, sin, and hate.

One day You came to dwell within.
You gave me peace where once there was sin.
Your love exceeded all my expectations
And brought about a great transformation.

You did for me what I was unable to do.
So now, Lord, I willingly give my life to You.
In a lifetime, You I could never repay.
But I will listen, Lord, and gladly obey.

If only there was a way without so much pain.
But now my life over sin I did regain.
You knew that was something You had to do.
For me, all that suffering You went through.

You gave Your best so there would be no lack.
You suffered the cross and stripes upon Your back.
You did not complain through all that pain.
It brought hope of eternal life once again.

Sin always kept me in defeat.
And caused me to be in constant retreat
Until Jesus came and showed me a better way.
Now my life is going in Your way today.

Thank You, Lord, for forgiving me.
Thank You, Lord, for setting me free.
Thank You, Lord, for coming to this earth.
Thank You, Lord, for my new birth.

Inspirational Poems of Encouragement

A FRIEND

I no longer walk in darkness,
Because I came to the Light.
Christ now lives within my heart,
You will help me through the battles to be fought.

Jesus said, "I will never leave or forsake you."
So what have I to fear?
Jesus is always there for you,
And will be every day.

Don't worry about tomorrow,
For I will take care of it for you.
Take up your cross and follow Me.
Because soon all the battles will be over.

Who is like unto Me?
Or who can be closer than a brother?
If you can find him, let Me know.
Can he save you; can he be a friend such as I?

Can anyone promise you tomorrow?
Can he extend your life?
I can tell you One that can,
And One that can promise more.

So cast all your cares upon Me,
I will see you through,
And while the battle is raging,
I will be there for you.

Now can you see, there is none like Me?
There is none to compare with Me.
So if you need a friend, come to me and see,
If I don't love you more than any other friend.

Is there a friend that would give his life for you?
Or, love you more than I.
Or, give you all that he has.
Then you have truly found a friend.

Inspirational Poems of Encouragement

ADAM AND JESUS

Out of the dust God created man,
Only one tree in the garden was there a ban.
Adam was created by God Almighty's hand,
He put him in the garden in a fruitful land.

Just tend the garden to Adam God did say,
He came to walk with him in the cool of the day.
I wish I knew how long innocence did last,
That part of man has now past.

Adam could have lived forever,
Disobeying God, their relationship it did sever.
Now in sin man would be,
He brought death to all, to you and me.

Would he do different if he could start again?
Now a new plan, in Christ it had to begin.
There was no other choice God could make,
His Son had to die for man's sake.

Adam was created to live forever;
Did God have in mind for him to die? Never.
Jesus, the second Adam was born to die;
Because Adam went along with the lie.

In Christ we are dead to sin,
In Him over death we shall win.
The apostles were there, His Word they heard,
We must believe what is written, it is His Word.

There is no other, Christ said, "I am the way."
Come to Him, make your decision today.
In preaching the gospel Christ was very bold.
His is the greatest story...the greatest story ever told.

Inspirational Poems of Encouragement

NEVER ENDING STORMS

The storms of life have beaten me down.
And they continue to pound and pound.
And the storms of time have taken their toll on me.
Surely, Lord, all this can't be hid from Thee.

The waters are getting so high,
And from me You go and hide, why?
How much more of this can I take?
Won't You come just for my sake?

The storms just keep coming.
And the sound of more keeps rumbling.
Won't the time ever come when these storms end?
Tell me Lord, on whom but You can I depend?

Lord, is there ever going to be a moment of relief?
I will take it even if it is very brief.
I wonder if it is worth even being alive;
Because I don't know if I will survive.

Oh, how I wish these storms would cease.
But they just seem to increase.
There seems to be no let-up to them at all.
Lord, somewhere did I miss Your call?

Give me the strength while these storms beat.
And to face them, never retreat.
The storms that lie ahead that I still must face;
I pray if one day at a time, You will give me grace.

If I go to be with You before these storms end,
A helping hand I know You will lend.
I know for me You have always been here.
When I thought You were far away, You were always near.

Inspirational Poems of Encouragement

JOY

You can have joy in your darkest hour,
When the enemy comes with all his power.
Happiness can go, but joy stays,
You can have joy all your days.

Joy is there when you are sad.
Joy is there when you are glad.
Joy doesn't leave because of circumstances,
And joy is not there just because of chances.

Joy is there when things go wrong,
In your heart there is still joy, and a song.
No one is able to take your joy from you.
Joy is there when the devil does all he can do.

Know in your heart there will be joy today
Share it with someone along the way.
Just let joy reign in your heart today,
Because joy is there to stay.

In life there will be sorrow as you go along,
But joy will put in your heart a new song.
Don't worry about tomorrow;
Joy is there even in the time of your sorrow.

There is no time like now to come to the giver of joy.
He had his beginning on earth as a baby boy;
But He grew up, died, and is alive.
And if needed, your joy He will gladly revive.

There is joy when you are up,
Full and running over is your cup.
There is joy when you are down,
Because joy always does abound.

Inspirational Poems of Encouragement

HOLY SPIRIT

Thank You , Holy Spirit, You are always near."
When I need You most, You say, I am here.
When hope seems to be slipping away,
You come and replace even more for that day.

Holy Spirit, I am glad You dwell within,
With You in my heart there is no room for sin.
Day by day, You show me the way,
You reveal to me my directions for the day.

The strong hold that I was facing today,
Holy Spirit, You help me as I go my way.
I want to listen to what You give me to say,
Maybe someone I could help today.

Holy Spirit, You know the need for speed,
In this world of doubt and greed.
Can't we see there is such a need?
The world with the gospel, we must feed.

There is much more yet to do,
And some of it is for me and you.
You help us with the race to be run.
At the finish line are the Father and the Son.

The way You always show,
So I will know.
If someone slips along the way,
Help me to help them, to start a new day.

Holy Spirit, You are welcome in me,
Because without You nothing would I be.
The things of Christ You reveal,
And to my heart God's Word You make real.

Inspirational Poems of Encouragement

A PURPOSE

Is there a purpose you were born?
To know God's will even when you are old and worn,
You are someone special, God loves you.
There is no one like you; God has a job to do.

There is so much yet to do.
Whether little or much it is required of me and you,
Did we take the time today to pray and read?
He will be there in testing time, in time of need.

There are many people that need someone to say,
God loves you, He cares; could I pray with you today?
There are some that just a hug will do.
You say I have no talent; God can still use you.

There is always the poor among us,
If God wants us to help, do we put up a fuss?
If we don't do the small things God might ask,
How could He trust us with a larger task?

Has God placed something on your heart to do?
God has a purpose; He has a plan for you,
You are the only one that can fulfill that plan,
You can do it; God knows you can.

I believe God had a purpose for words that would rhyme,
They say God loves them; He is with you all the time,
So I write down the words God gives to me,
I pray it would help the one God meant for it to be.

Yes ,there is a purpose God has for you,
God will always reveal His will, too.
Fulfill the plan God has for you,
He will help you with the job you are to do.

Inspirational Poems of Encouragement

BY IT

Your Word to my life, Lord, is a delight.
Somewhere, someone is reading it day and night.
By it people are discovering salvation,
And it has become a new revelation.

It reveals God's will for man.
By it we know man can't save himself; only Christ can.
As we study it, its words have more meaning.
And each day becomes more revealing.

No book can take the place of the Bible.
It is God's Word, and what it says is reliable.
It reveals God's love for all mankind.
And the good things for us He has in mind.

One day we will be judged by His Word.
We must tell it until all have heard.
You can be encouraged by it.
Making it part of your life; you will benefit.

It will teach you God's ways.
It will guide you all of your days.
By it we learn of God's grace.
And life's problems alone we do not have to face.

It shows how to be ready on judgment day.
It tells you Christ is the way.
It informs us about Heaven and hell.
It's a choice you must make – where you wish to dwell.

There is nothing you can compare it to.
The truth about God it reveals to you.
It has the answer. It is what God and the prophets say.
Live by it until God calls you home or caught away.

Inspirational Poems of Encouragement

HE ALWAYS KNEW

When I was unlovable, You were there;
When I deserved judgment, You were always fair,
All I deserved was hell.
My spirit You healed, now I am well.

When I was in sin, You set me free.
When I did not love You, You came to me.
You loved me, and with me You want to be.
My eyes You opened that I might see.

Lord, from You my sins I tried to hide.
While in sin, You could not come in and abide.
You saw what I was trying to do;
But You said if you repent I will come to you.

I know my ungodly ways grieved You so,
And every sin of mine You did always know.
I could never hide them from You,
You changed my life; show me what to do.

Even my thoughts You always knew,
My spirit You always wanted to renew.
Why did I wait so long to hear Your voice?
Why did I wait so long to make You my choice?

All the secret things I did;
From You I could not keep them hid.
My ungodly ways You always knew,
Repent, that's what You said I must do.

Lord, thank You for what You did for me,
So I can be all You want me to be.
Help me to walk humbly before Thee,
There are those I must tell; it is required of me.

Inspirational Poems of Encouragement

I KNOW

I know when you hurt,
The evil that comes I avert.
I know when things are bad,
And the hard times you have had.

I know when you are awake and want to sleep,
Be not disheartened; you, I safely keep.
I know of the worries you are going through,
And your disappointments, too.

I know of the times you are upset with Me,
And the way you wish things would be.
I know you wish a change I would make,
And all your troubles from you take.

I know you think, what more can go wrong?
Why have You let this go on so long?
I know you wish the rapture would take place,
So tomorrow you would not have to face.

You think I am not answering when you pray,
That I am not listening to what you say.
You think your troubles are getting too big for Me,
Everything you go through I know and see.

I know there are things you wish you knew,
And things you would like to forget, too.
Heaven, that you have longed for, you will see,
Then no more suffering there will be.

I know what you have been through,
I understand; I had My time of suffering, too.
When on your face you fall down flat,
The devil still didn't win; God saw to that.

Inspirational Poems of Encouragement

WHY?

Why has it been so long since from You I heard?
Why is this not mentioned in Your Word?
Why, to me, do You no longer talk?
Why won't You come and with me walk?

Why do You stay so far away?
Why won't You come and visit me today?
Why do You no longer say, "I love you?"
Why is there nothing more You will do?

Why do I feel so helpless and down?
Why is it You no longer come around?
Why won't You, once again, lift me up?
Why can't I drink from Your refreshing cup?

Why do I have to walk this path alone?
Why can't a little of Your joy be shown?
Why do You not listen when I ask?
Why is just living becoming such a task?

Why is it You no longer care about me?
Why is this the way things must be?
Why is there no answer when I pray?
Why is the answer never now, today?

Why don't You touch my hurting soul?
Why is all this taking its toll?
Why is there nothing when, after You, I yearn?
Why do You not show me of Your concern?

"I have seen everything you have gone through.
Not for one minute, alone, have I left you.
I have seen your every "why".
I came to give you life, grace and to die."

Inspirational Poems of Encouragement

LOVE

Love has always been.
Love rejoices when, a new life, you begin.
Love does not seek its own.
Love never leaves you alone.

Love will be with you all the way;
Through your ups and downs, and your every day.
Love is there when things go wrong;
When you are weak and when you are strong.

Love stands up for what is right.
Love will help you through your longest night.
Love stays close when friends forsake you.
Love will be there while waiting for your breakthrough.

Love never fails.
Love will guide you when the storms of life assails.
Love will get you through your darkest hour.
Love is a mighty power.

Love is there when you get old.
Love will keep you until Christ's face you behold.
You can even love your enemy.
Try God's love, you will see.

Love is manifested in our lives each day;
By the way we act ,what we do and say.
Love like this was never known,
Until Jesus left all His glory and His throne.

Love was shown on the cross when Jesus died.
Of His love, the prophets testified.
Each day His love, with us, He shares.
It just shows how very much He cares.

Inspirational Poems of Encouragement

GRACE

God's grace does abound.
In your tribulation, grace can be found;
And always plenty to go around,
But does not come by the pound.

Grace is for all to receive,
When on God's Son, you believe.
When it seems all hope is gone,
God will give you grace. You can go on!

Adam chose death instead of life.
Upon all he brought sin, death and strife.
Adam, God would still forgive,
And gave him grace so he could live.

No one sees the crisis you are going through.
No one knows about it but you.
You think, alone these things you must face.
God will be there with more than enough grace.

For grace, I have not fought.
And, with money, it cannot be bought.
Grace did not come by work that I wrought;
But when, after Jesus, I sought.

In the time of troubles that I had to face,
God so freely gave me His grace.
Now into His love and grace I have tapped;
And by grace set free from sin, where I was trapped.

"My grace is sufficient", Jesus said;
"To those who know I'm alive and not dead.
There is nothing too hard you will ever face,
That you can't overcome by My grace."

When the mountains you are facing seem so high,
You think they reach the sky.
But when there is a need for more,
To grace, God will always have an open door.

Inspirational Poems of Encouragement

THE GOOD NEWS

Where Christ walked and preached we now must go,
Because the good news, He wants everyone to know.
Unless we take the good news to everyone,
They will never hear of God's Son.

Be not afraid to take the good news,
To those far and near and the abused.
Christ will be with you all the way,
He will never forsake you, not for one day.

To you, God's Word I gave,
And if they repent, I will save.
There are some that hear and will not obey,
What I have commanded, what I say.

It is not My will that any should perish,
Because every soul I love and cherish.
The good news must be proclaimed to all,
I don't want one soul to be lost or fall.

Are we getting the good news to all?
Everyone must hear. It is our call.
There are so many dying that have not heard,
Take them the good news; take them God's Word.

Go and tell everyone Jesus cried,
Have we done our best, have we really tried?
With everyone working, the job will get done,
And by the good news, sin they must shun.

Go and tell all nations what I have said,
I have risen, I am not dead.
Every minute counts, every minute you must use,
Go and tell them, tell them the good news.

Inspirational Poems of Encouragement

I'M JUST NOT SURE

If there was no mercy, I would have perished long ago.
I was a sinner, but that You know.
But You came and died for man,
Why, I'm just not sure I understand.

Because of Your mercy I am still here to praise Thee,
And perhaps the rapture I also will see.
You came to give life to man,
Why, I'm just not sure I understand.

Man has rejected, rebelled; yet mercy You still show.
From Heaven to the cross You did go.
From the beginning, mercy You have shown to man.
Why, I'm just not sure I understand.

Your mercy You show to all generations,
Because You love the people of all nations.
From the beginning, You never gave up on man.
Why, I'm just not sure I understand.

Man has done everything contrary to Your will,
Yet You love him, You love him still.
All the hate toward You, You still love man,
Why, I'm just not sure I understand.

All that will; You are waiting for them to come,
You want everyone to have life, everyone!
You did everything needed to save man,
Why, I'm just not sure I understand.

Satan was given dominion over the earth,
Man was in sin and needed a new birth.
So You came and gave Your life for man,
And made such a change in me, now I understand.

Inspirational Poems of Encouragement

NEW BEGINNINGS

The new millennium is now here,
Do you wish it could be without a care?
Your love and fears with Jesus you can share,
Who knows, maybe His coming will be this year.

This year, don't we wish we knew what lay ahead?
Jesus knows, He is alive, He is not dead.
The people of the nations to Christ must be led,
His Word to all people must be read.

In Jesus the blows of satan we are able to fend,
Those preaching the gospel we must send.
In Jesus we must trust, on Him we can depend.
This year, His flock we must tend.

What do we have in mind for this New Year?
Will we help the poor, pray and shed a tear?
In Jesus there is nothing to fear,
He is waiting to help, He really does care.

In the New Year we need to share,
Get the gospel to those far and near.
Many are living in bondage, who live in fear.
Tell them about Jesus, the one that is so dear.

Maybe this year will be a new beginning for you.
Jesus will do for you what no one else can do.
Look in His Word, His Word is true.
Without His death there was no hope for you.

Jesus is waiting at the door of your heart.
Won't you let Him in, He will never depart.
Let this year be for you a new start,
Come to Jesus, and Heaven you will be a part.

Inspirational Poems of Encouragement

PEARL OF GREAT PRICE

Your life before God and man hasn't been very nice,
But God thinks you are a pearl of great price.
The potential in you God could see.
But your life wasn't the way He meant for it to be.

From beginning to end He saw your life.
It would be filled with bitterness and strife.
He knew of the sorrow and pain.
He even knew a new life in Him you would begin.

He knew of the good times and the bad.
He knew the ups and mostly downs you have had.
He saw your life laden with sin,
And knew there was no peace within.

Death started following you around.
It stayed close but didn't make a sound.
God knew what sin would do.
If only you could realize it, too.

He knew sin was taking its toll on you,
But a change you were not ready to do.
He saw the things going on that should not be.
He just wished all this you could see.

If no change you were on a path of no return,
But sin was like a flame that had to burn.
He saw what a grip it had on you.
He would wait and see what you decided to do.

You finally realized the results of sin,
And asked Jesus to come and dwell within.
Now you are that pearl of great worth,
And have now experienced the new birth.

Inspirational Poems of Encouragement

COMING BACK

Because of sin Jesus died,
He rose, now He is glorified.
On the cross His blood was shed,
After three days God raised Him from the dead.

To the poor the gospel was preached,
And to the sick and suffering He reached.
In our time of hurts Jesus cares,
When we call He hears.

The reason Jesus died, I am to blame,
To change lives like mine, is why He came.
He then told His disciples I must go away,
But I will be coming back one day.

In our hearts Jesus now lives,
And when we grieve Him He forgives.
He's alive and never more to die,
Soon He will be coming back in the sky.

Jesus is the same, He still heals,
And unto us His will He reveals.
One day He is coming back for me,
His face I will finally get to see.

On the cross Jesus cried,
Father, forgive them, He said, before He died.
By His death we are set free,
One day with Him we will forever be.

Many times Jesus went away alone and prayed,
And in His Father's will He stayed.
On the throne beside the Father He now sits,
For us, the devil He always outwits.

Inspirational Poems of Encouragement

THAT OLD TREE

Jesus died that day for me;
So from sin, I can be free.
If we are faithful, one day we will see,
The One that died on that old tree.

God's heart must have ached that day,
To see His Son suffer that way.
No other way could it be done for me;
He must die on that old tree.

That day of His death has come and gone.
It wasn't even Him that did the wrong.
It was my sins. It was me,
That caused Him to die on that old tree.

God saw sin would forever keep us apart;
And it broke His heart.
Something had to be done for me.
So He died on that old tree.

Oh the terrible price He paid!
This was the decision they had made.
This is the way it had to be.
He must die on that old tree.

So much suffering He went through!
Oh how He loved me and you!
A new life He has given me,
Because He died on that old tree.

If that old tree could, would it say,
"I don't want this man to die on me today!"
And would Jesus kindly reply,
"On you, today, I must die"?

Inspirational Poems of Encouragement

LORD I GIVE YOU PRAISE

Lord, we just come before You with praise,
As we travel down this life of uncertain maze.
And for all the things for us that You do,
I bow my knees and worship You.

Let praise in my heart always be,
Because of Your love and care for me.
Before You, Lord, my voice I will raise.
The devil hates for me to come with praise.

With our praise we drive the devil crazy.
So to him everything will be hazy.
Because of the words in rhyme You have given me,
In them, I just want to praise and glorify Thee.

I want to praise You in everything I do.
I know it is all because of You.
It was for me Your life You gave,
Sinners like me You came to save.

No other sacrifice would do for me.
You looked down and You could see
That from the devil I could not flee.
You said, Father, a sacrifice for him I will be.

How can I ever praise You for all You did?
My sins from You were never hid.
So I want to say thank You once again.
For all You went through and what You did.

Lord, I give You praise
For getting me through life's tangled maze.
And from following my own ways,
Now and forever Lord, I give You praise.

Inspirational Poems of Encouragement

TROUBLES EVERYWHERE

Is there trouble all around?
And where there is, Grace does abound.
Are you weary from climbing that mountain?
Come and be refreshed and drink at His fountain.

Are you going through a desert hot and dry?
Do you sometimes feel you want to cry?
Does it seem you are at the end of your road?
And things happening are such a heavy load?

Are your problems getting bigger by the day?
Jesus is near; for you a great price He had to pay.
Are things being said about you that are not true?
Jesus hears everything, He knows what to do.

Do you wonder about things you are going through?
You aren't the only one; many others also do.
Does it seem you are being knocked down?
Jesus is close, He can be found.

When things get where no more you can bear,
Jesus will help, your burden He will share.
You might be weary to the bone,
But never again will you have to walk alone.

Does it seem no one else has trouble like yours,
And then even more occurs?
Is the cross heavy that is on your back?
Jesus will see you have no lack.

Do you wish you knew what lies ahead?
Come to Jesus, He is alive, He is not dead.
Do you wish a new song would arise in your heart?
Maybe today there can be a new start.

Inspirational Poems of Encouragement

WEARY TO THE BONE

Have the dregs of life filled your cup,
And you are down more than you are up?
Lord, the rut I am in I just seem to stay.
It has just been another miserable day.

No one sees the mess I am in,
No one is able to help, not my family or my kin.
The things in my life are up to my chin,
Nothing I try, or do, I can't seem to win.

It seems there is no right way to turn.
For things to be better, I do yearn.
But no matter how hard I try,
Crying never seems to help, but I still cry.

Is there left no joy, is there no peace?
My sorrow, my pains will it ever cease?
Is this all there is to life?
Is it always toils and strife?

Can't I find just a little peace and rest?
Is this all there is, is this the best?
Must I stay weary to the bone?
Must I wish I had never been born?

Is there a way out of what I am going through?
Is there anyone to help, can any tell me what to do?
Yes, there is someone, Jesus is His name.
He is Lord of today and forever. He is the same.

Lord, I have been told I could come to You,
That You care, and would know what to do.
Now, Lord, I turn my miserable life over to You,
Because I sure don't know what else to do.

Inspirational Poems of Encouragement

MY DILEMMA

Lord, You see what a dilemma I am in.
Nothing like this happened, even when I was in sin.
I hope this doesn't last too long,
Or I believe my mind will be gone.

I have never faced anything like this before.
What will I do, if there is even more?
Lord, I need You to help me out of this mess.
If anything in my life grieves You, Lord, I confess.

Maybe someone could come and tell me what to do,
Or Lord, is there someone with a message from You?
I don't know how much more of this I can take.
But this I know; You will not forsake.

It seems every day that goes by,
Things get worse, and I don't even know why.
Lord, I can't seem to do anything but cry.
But to forsake You…never, I would rather die!

Besides there is no one else I can turn to.
I have always put my trust in You.
But if I must, I will wait.
Long ago into Your hands I committed my fate.

At Your timing I will be waiting for Your reply.
You know what is best, even if I do ask You why.
In the meantime, I will seek You and pray.
The answer will come; maybe now it is on the way.

I see everything you are going through;
Anything you go through, I will be with you.
Stay on the course; one day from this you will be free.
All because you kept your trust in Me.

Inspirational Poems of Encouragement

DESPERATE CALL

Lord, I know what is expected of me.
To write poems, in them You will always be.
Help me to listen to what You want me to say,
To help those that are discouraged today.

There are times you feel so discouraged and afraid.
You wonder if you can make it up the next grade.
The things in your life that are going on,
You sure need a touch; it seems it has been so long.

You feel God has cast you aside.
You are not even sure if in Him you any longer abide.
In your heart you have thought of giving up,
Heavy has been the load; empty has been your cup.

You are so tired and weary,
And everything in your life has been going contrary.
There seems to be no help to be found.
Your troubles just keep mounting; they just abound.

You wish you could get a visit from the Rock of Ages.
"I will never leave you" (it is written) on the pages.
It seems there is no hope left for you.
You wish things in your life would change soon, too.

Lord, how much more of this can I take?
It seems I am praying whenever I am awake.
If there is a reason You don't come,
I need Your presence and grace, give me some.

I have heard your desperate call.
You will certainly make it; you will not fall.
I have already taken care of things for you.
Because I still have more for you to do.

Inspirational Poems of Encouragement

TOMORROW

Each day is just another day of hurt for me.
If anyone knew I think they would agree.
I wish there would be a better day,
But I know it won't turn out that way.

Oh, if tomorrow wouldn't have to be so bad,
Plenty days of pain and grief I have had.
This day of hurt, will vanish without a trace.
Then tomorrow, again these things I must face.

I never had someone I could call my best friend,
And if there was, it always soon would end.
Why does it always have to turn out this way?
Just another cruel day.

Will I ever see a brighter tomorrow,
That isn't filled with so much pain and sorrow?
I already know the pain tomorrow will hold.
I will be reminded; I will be told.

Will there ever be a little ray of hope?
Through another tomorrow will I be able to cope?
Will better times ever come?
Good days, will there ever be some?

Tomorrow will just bring bitterness and strife.
That is the way it has been all of my life.
How can I expect it to be different now for me?
When I already know exactly the way it will be?

There is a better life in Jesus, my friend.
He is my friend and our friendship is yet to end.
Ask Him to come and be your friend,
And best of all, your relationship will never end.

Inspirational Poems of Encouragement

JESUS

Jesus is the one who suffered and died.
It was for us He was crucified.
He heard my cry and forgave me of my sin.
Now He can dwell within.

When I had no hope Jesus came,
I caused Him to die, I am to blame.
He forgives when I grieve Him, He says I love you.
With all my failures, He still brought me through.

When you need Jesus, He will be there.
Satan wants you to believe Jesus does not care.
He is our enemy; he is our foe,
Jesus also comes and satan has to go.

When your troubles come by the truckload,
Jesus says, don't worry, in you I have made my abode.
When there is so much sorrow and you need more grace,
Satan alone we do not have to face.

Jesus preached the gospel to all that would hear,
And to all that obeyed He would draw near.
Today we still have his Word
That was passed on to us by those that heard.

In His Word miracles took place day after day,
To see Him manifested we must obey.
Then we will be rewarded on judgment day,
All because the price for sin Jesus did already pay.

Tomorrow might be too late, come to Jesus now.
He will forgive you even if you don't know how.
He has His arms outstretched to you,
He can change your life, the thing no one else can do.

Inspirational Poems of Encouragement

THE WAY IT HAD TO BE

The curse must be broken at any cost,
Something must be done; the human race was lost.
To free man, Christ would have to die.
Oh, if there was some other way, He would try.

The curse was strong this He saw,
Man must be delivered from the curse of the law.
God saw that no other way would do,
His Son would have to die, this He did for you.

On Calvary's hill His hands were nailed to the tree.
So that from sin and the curse I could be free.
Cursed is everyone that hangs on a tree,
This is the only way; this is the way it had to be.

Cursed are they that keep not all the law, Moses said.
Christ came to fulfill the law, no longer is He dead.
Now we know the curse could be broken,
Christ fulfilled the word about Him that was spoken.

God grieved to see what His Son would go through,
But He loved us so much; He was willing to do.
Can you imagine such love as His?
So to break the curse, this is the way it is.

A good plan the Lord had sought,
From the curse, for us Christ has brought.
Now rejoice because you are set free.
It was the way it had to be.

So He came to this earth to die,
Sin was the reason why.
Into the future He could see,
This is the way it had to be.

Inspirational Poems of Encouragement

WHEN LORD?

When Lord, are You going to listen to my cry?
Will it not be until I am caught away or until I die?
Long ago into Your hands I placed my fate.
When I pray, why must I have to wait, and wait?

There are others that say the same.
They also love You and call upon Your name.
Why must I have to wait so long?
If I continue, will You be there at dawn?

Won't You come now in answer to my prayer?
I know You personally and I know You care.
So Lord, those that call upon Your name,
Come with Your healing touch, You are the same.

Lord, I come before You each day,
Why do You not hear me when I pray?
Why do You not listen to what I have to say?
At least give me peace along the way.

Let me say, never give up or quit.
Jesus might visit you in just a little bit.
What is there any way to go back to?
Your breakthrough might be today, and Jesus waiting for you.

So stay steadfast, His timing is always best.
During your time of waiting He will give you rest.
He always has the right answer for you,
And what He gives you is always the best, too.

There was a long period I went through,
And there was nothing about it I could do.
But still I continued to pray.
One day my breakthrough came and oh, what a special day!

Inspirational Poems of Encouragement

NEVER TOO OLD

Those silver threads in your hair, is it now all white?
Just remember you have been God's light.
And that light must continue to shine,
Because Christ says you are mine.

You're older and think there is nothing I can do.
God needs me; He needs you.
The hurting need a kind word from you today.
Others having a difficult day; for them you could pray.

The devil would like for you to believe you are through,
And there is nothing more for God you can do.
We are not too old for God to use, one and all.
He will speak; on your life He has placed a call.

Just be available; God will send someone by.
Maybe all they need is a smile, a hug or a "hi".
Someone discouraged God might send your way.
Or God might send you to visit them today.

Now that you are older your wisdom is so in need.
Giving good advice for the day can be your good deed
God will give you wisdom in what to do or say.
Your words can help those struggling along the way.

Don't worry if today He doesn't send someone by,
There is someone God has heard their desperate cry.
Just trust in God and pray,
Maybe a wayward soul you can help today.

God never thinks you are too old to be used.
He needs you to help the lonely and the abused.
You are God's child and He really loves you.
There is so much left for God you can do.

Inspirational Poems of Encouragement

BROKEN SPIRIT

From a youth you have really had a hard time,
You have been told you are not worth a dime.
Jesus never looks at it that way.
God loves you; a great price He had to pay.

You will never amount to anything, you are told.
They want to fit and keep you in their mold.
Jesus never looks at it that way.
A better life He wants to give you today.

They say you never do anything right,
And you are worthless; I want you out of my sight.
Jesus never looks at it that way.
You are someone special He would say.

You are not worth the salt that goes in your bread.
And oh, how it hurts when these things are said.
Jesus never looks at it that way.
I love you, so does it matter what they say?

There will never be anyone in your life to care.
There is no one their life with you will share.
Jesus never looks at it that way.
He will gladly give you someone special today.

Things will always be as they have been for you,
Regardless of what you think or try to do.
Jesus never looks at it that way.
For you He will give you a new beginning today.

After all those lies you have been told,
And on them all you have been sold.
From all these things you can be free.
Jesus says, come to Me.

Inspirational Poems of Encouragement

IS LIFE WORTH LIVING?

Lord, at times it seems You do not care,
And it can sure give us a scare.
When we pray, we think You do not hear,
Sometimes these things can lead to fear.

Why at times all alone do we feel?
Come, touch us with Your tender hand and heal.
Won't You come and speak, won't You come today?
You have the answer; You know what to say.

Has life for you been so unforgiving,
That taking your life is far better than living?
Believe me it is not,
Christ loves you, He cares. You mean you forgot?

Many believe their hurts are from You,
And that is what You want to do.
It was because of our sins that You died,
Stripes were put on Your back; a spear pierced Your side.

For many all their lives has been turmoil and pain,
They think their lives they will never regain.
Others just wish they knew which way to turn,
And to find relief from their troubles they do yearn.

Hearing about things others are going through,
Christ in His timing will be there for you.
If you think from you God's face He has hid,
Remember what Christ went through, this for you He did.

Has life chewed you up and spit you out,
And there is nothing left but fear and doubt?
Come to Jesus, He is so merciful and forgiving,
He will give you a new life; then life will be worth living.

Inspirational Poems of Encouragement

AMERICA

America, the greatest country on earth,
And has been since the day of its birth.
People come to find freedom to worship God,
And claimed America everywhere their feet trod.

America reaches out to those that want a better life,
Because all they have known are toils and strife.
To all religions America is still free,
America is the country where many want to be.

Many have fought and died to keep America free,
But is America today what God wants Her to be?
From America to more people has the gospel gone,
Have we failed God; where have we gone wrong?

Out of our schools was taken the Bible and the right to pray,
Our homes and schools are the places they need to stay.
Those in authority to remove out of our schools the Bible,
On the Day of Judgment will God hold them liable?

Let us not forget the good America does that is right.
We help others have freedom; we go and fight.
America gives to other countries that are in need,
And many nations the hungry we help feed.

Many would come to America, if they had the chance,
Bits of paper about it, they longingly glance.
But, has America forgotten its Godly past?
Then how can our great nation last?

America, its roots we must never forget.
Until everyone hears the gospel we must never quit,
America, we must listen to God's call,
And God bless America, the greatest land of all.

Inspirational Poems of Encouragement

DECISION

Don't be fooled by false preaching.
Listen to what Christ said, follow His teaching.
He will never lead you astray.
It took His life for your sins to pay.

Jesus came and died for you, for all,
And is just waiting for you to call.
So call upon Him now, make it today.
You can't go wrong, He said, "I am the way."

The broad way, the narrow way, one you must choose,
If the narrow way, Christ, you cannot lose.
No one can make this decision, but you.
This alone you have to do.

The decision you make decides your hereafter.
It can be love, joy and laughter.
The right decision can be a bright tomorrow.
The wrong one can lead to death and sorrow.

Have you made your decision for your eternity?
I have made it for me.
It will be the best decision you will ever make.
Your eternity is at stake.

There is joy in Heaven when you repent.
It will be the best few minutes you ever spent.
It will bring joy and peace,
And life that will never cease.

If you make the decision for Christ, you will be glad.
And it will make satan mad.
With Jesus, you won't have to worry.
Make your decision soon…hurry.

Inspirational Poems of Encouragement

WISDOM

Lord, give me wisdom so I will be wise;
To discern, when things come in disguise.
And always know when it is of Thee.
Wisdom, Lord, give to me.

Wisdom was with You from the start.
You and wisdom have never been apart.
So let Thy wisdom from me flow,
That I might help others grow.

Wisdom is of old,
And is far more precious than silver or gold.
Wisdom will do everything it can,
To bring God's best to man.

Wisdom goes back far before time;
The creation You helped God design.
Heaven and things great and small;
By wisdom, You created them all.

Make wisdom part of your daily life.
Live by wisdom and free from strife.
For wisdom there is no price;
But it will give you good advice.

You are given wisdom to get wealth;
And to know what is good for your health.
Keep wisdom close to your breast;
And God will take care of all the rest.

If any lack wisdom, let him ask.
It will be given to do God's task.
With wisdom you will surely reap;
And on you, good things God will heap.

Thank you for the wisdom you have given me;
And in all things I will glorify Thee,
To be all that I can be, so I can hear,
"Well done!" when I stand before Thee.

Inspirational Poems of Encouragement

WHAT AM I HERE FOR?

What on earth are you here for?
Sit around, have a good time, or,
Fulfill the call God has given you.
He would not ask if His call you could not do.

If each of us will do our little bit:
Tell what God did, all your sins He did remit.
So all will know Christ came to save man.
Who can get this good news to the world? We can.

Do you think you're here for your own pleasure? No.
Christ said, "Into all the world you must go…"
There are so many that have not heard;
We must get to them God's Word.

If we can't go, then someone we must send:
A little of our time and helping hand we can lend.
Unless we take the opportunity God gives me and you,
How will those that have not heard know what to do?

The very best Heaven had, God gave.
The world is lost. Tell them, "Christ came to save."
We will be held accountable on that day,
If we fail to show the wayward soul the way.

God gives each of us a mission.
He will show you. Open your heart and listen.
If we fail the world will die in sin.
I know, because there I once have been.

Tell your loved ones and the world Jesus cares.
He came and died; His love to all He shares.
So what on earth am I here to do?
Reach the lost, help the poor…it's required of me and you.

Inspirational Poems of Encouragement

PROMISES

Is your joy and peace completely gone?
Does it seem it has been that way so long?
Keep your trust in the One that cannot fail,
One that will keep you when life's storms assail.

He does not make a promise He will not keep.
He promises if you are faithful you will reap.
You can have the promise of the life that now is,
And eternal life to all that are His.

On His Word you can rely,
And none of His promises He will deny.
Never be afraid to ask;
Your needs are not that great a task.

Come boldly to the throne of grace.
In Him all your troubles you can face.
He will be there in your time of need.
Ask, believe. You don't have to beg or plead.

The promises are yours if in His Word they are said.
Get His Word in your heart, not just in your head.
Trust in, depend on what is said in His Word.
Don't always rely on just what you have heard.

Take time each day for His Word and pray,
When things go wrong, in His Word you must stay.
See if there isn't a promise just for you.
Ask and see what God will do.

Don't be discouraged when the devil comes to say:
"God won't keep His promises, not any day."
We know God's promises are sure.
His Word is timeless, ageless and pure.

Inspirational Poems of Encouragement

YOUR LAST DAY

Your last day to live could be today or tonight.
Maybe sin has been your delight.
Maybe no longer will you live,
And your sins you have not asked Jesus to forgive.

Maybe you have heard the gospel time and again
And now it is almost too late to repent of sin,
But not if you come now to Him.
A new life Christ gives; not the way it has been.

Satan wants to keep you under his power.
Christ wants to change that, even at this late hour.
Come; see what a change He will make.
Leaving Christ out of your life can be a big mistake.

Has life without Christ given you peace?
Christ gives peace, and life that will not cease.
He will give you life beyond anything you can compare,
And that life with you He wants to share.

Christ, at your last hour wants to save you.
His family He wants to welcome you into.
The joy He gives lasts forever.
And death cannot sever.

Maybe you have once tasted that the Lord is good,
And you have not repented, knowing you should.
Maybe your time to die has now come,
And you are not ready to face the Just One.

Has life brought you nothing but pain and grief?
You think taking your life is the only way for relief.
Ask Jesus into your heart, He is so forgiving.
He wants you to live; He will make life worth living.

Come, let Him make your life clean.
It will be better than anything you have ever seen.
The thief on the cross asked Jesus to forgive,
And that day with Christ in Paradise began to live.

Inspirational Poems of Encouragement

LORD GOD ALMIGHTY

I am the Lord God Almighty,
I am not petty or flighty.
I do not take matters lightly,
I look after my creation daily and nightly.

There was a purpose behind each thing I did,
Nothing good from man did I keep hid.
I had a plan; what I wanted him to do,
Before the creation I had already thought of you.

I created man to live in peace;
I gave him life that would never cease.
But man chose death, by the decision he made,
Now a price for sin had to be paid.

Into the world Christ came to bring light,
It is now up to man to choose wrong or right.
There is no longer an excuse for sin,
All must come to Him to enter in.

He gives life to all that will come,
Eternal life He offers to everyone.
Your life He wants to change,
Life for death, don't you want to exchange?

His love is far greater than you know.
In sin why do you continue to go?
He reaches down to where you are,
For me that was very far.

The decision is still yours to make.
Sin will catch up with you, make no mistake.
In the new earth only righteousness will reign,
Christ will be here, never will there be sin again.

Inspirational Poems of Encouragement

WHAT IF HE HAD SAID NO?

Jesus died; He took my place,
Not just for me, but the whole human race.
God said, "Son, it is now time for You to go."
But what if He had said no?

So to the earth Jesus came,
My life has not been the same.
By His coming we can defeat our foe…
But what if He had said no?

Our sins forced Him to come,
Man was doomed, He must die; that is the sum,
All because He loved us so…
But what if He had said no?

God knew no one else would do.
That's why He gave His life for me, for you.
So to the cross He had to go…
But what if He had said no?

He had always been with the Father, He must leave.
To see His Son go, surely His heart, it did grieve.
So He came to the earth below.
But what if He had said no?

God gave us the very best He had.
He died for the good; He died for the bad.
No greater love on me could He bestow,
But what if He had said no?

I'm so glad Jesus came.
He changed my life. I have not been the same.
All because He loved me so,
And I'm so glad He did not say no!

Inspirational Poems of Encouragement

HOLD ON TO YOUR FAITH

Does it seem those around you are doing fine?
And your troubles keep mounting all the time.
You may never know what they are going through;
Remember they have problems, too.

How long since your prayer has been heard?
Hold on to the promises that are in His Word.
Your situation is different to you it seems,
Jesus will help you, for He has the means.

Does it seem there is never any joy and peace,
And the things going on in your life never cease?
Hold on, your blessing might come on the morrow,
Then you can help others in their time of sorrow.

Do things in your past still haunt you?
You tried everything, and don't know what else to do.
When satan keeps reminding you of your past,
Remind him of his future, his troubles will always last.

Does every day turn out bad?
You are so depressed and sad,
You hope there will be a better day tomorrow,
And all it did was bring more sorrow.

Does it seem you are driven right into the ground,
And you are so far down you will never be found?
Jesus knows exactly where you are.
Hold on to your faith, you will be better off by far.

Are the dark clouds in your life beginning to form?
And then without warning there is a storm.
If they have persecuted Me, they will persecute you.
But I will be with you always, I will see you through.

Inspirational Poems of Encouragement

SURVIVING LIFE'S STORMS

The storms in my life seem so unfair,
And the days that are good sure are rare.
If there is a God, He sure must not be seeing me,
The things that hurt me all my life He would see.

Are things going to continue this same way?
Why Lord do You not hear what I have to say?
Every way I turn there is another dilemma I must face,
Am I alone facing this out of the whole human race?

It seems I have never had a friend to care,
So is there anyone my troubles I can share?
Lord, will You listen and help me today,
To find a friend to walk with me along the way?

Isn't there anyone I can tell my hurts to?
Is it going to stay and nothing I can do?
Lord, won't You come, won't you look my way?
And give me a little relief from my troubles today.

I am so tired and worn.
These storms make me weary and torn.
I have heard somewhere of Job's woes,
His pain did not last forever, on and on mine goes.

The time will come when Jesus you will meet.
Joy will come and your despair you will defeat.
Your spirit will be renewed; it will revive,
You will make it; you will survive.

I can't talk to you so this poem will have to do.
I don't know the pain you are going through,
I know Jesus will come; He will be there for you.
He was there for me; He will be there for you, too.

Inspirational Poems of Encouragement

SILENT

Lord I heard about You at a very young age.
I listened as Your Word was read from each page.
Jesus, I know from God You were sent.
And of my sins I did repent.

Lord Your presence I now need to feel.
Won't You come touch me and heal?
Have I done wrong, is that why You are so quiet?
Are You going to stay silent yet another night?

Why do You not come when I ask?
Is listening to me become a task?
Is there no answer when I pray?
Are You going to stay silent still another day?

Is this the way You want things to stay?
Don't You want our relationship better than this way?
Must I be the only one with something to say,
While You remain silent night and day?

Are You not going to speak to me anymore?
Has my seeking You become a bore?
Is what was between us over, is it gone?
Lord why have You been silent so long?

There was so much we used to talk about.
Things about my life, is there now some doubt?
Is there more than I am that I should be?
Then break the silence and speak to me.

Why were your thoughts that I do not care?
All this time My blessing with you I did share.
When you called I heard. I saw each tear.
I was always there, you just didn't realize how near.

Inspirational Poems of Encouragement

BEING LIKE THIS

Lord do You not know what it is like to be depressed?
Why You never came I have guessed and guessed.
I called but You did not hear.
You just turned a deaf ear.

Lord what more can I do?
Must I wait forever on You?
Others, their prayers You have heard.
You do not answer when I pray and get into Your Word.

Why do You continue to make me wait?
Being like this I sure do hate.
You let things stay this same way.
You don't come; that means waiting another day.

Is there nothing more for me You will do?
You know being like this is torment to go through.
Why do You turn Your face from me?
Do You not want to look at the torment You will see?

Lord, there are things I just can't understand.
Since You are almighty and compass sea and land.
You have overlooked me all these years.
I am left depressed and fighting these fears.

Won't You come now and touch me?
So from this torment I can be free.
You see what is going on, yet make me wait.
Maybe You aren't coming at all, or running late.

You have been faithful, I know of your wait.
I will be there; I never run late.
There will be many now you can help along the way.
You are now prepared; you will be wise in what to say.

Inspirational Poems of Encouragement

INDEPENDENCE DAY

For our independence a great army they fought,
And by God's hand a miracle was wrought.
Fight was the only way they could see,
To get independence; this is the way it had to be.

So they fought and won,
Whether by sword, bayonet or gun.
They fought for our liberty.
They fought so America could be free.

On July 4, 1776, was our first Independence Day.
A price for freedom they were willing to pay.
It was hard fighting back in those days,
America must be free to follow God's ways.

With a ragtag army God beat our foe,
Maybe the purpose, the people did not know.
The Gospel God wanted America to preach,
Now, those that have not heard we must reach.

We weren't there on our first Independence Day;
We still fight to keep it that way.
Now America has departed from Your way.
Lord, come forgive America of her sins, don't delay.

America must return to what You called her to do.
Lest we lose favor with You.
If America forgets You and goes her own way,
How much longer will we celebrate Independence Day?

People that came thought America was a land of bliss,
But you see God had a hand in all this.
Today we celebrate Independence Day,
And I pray this is the way it will always stay.

Inspirational Poems of Encouragement

SIN

Where Christ once dwelt is there now sin,
Where once was peace, is it now emptiness within?
Christ and sin, both you cannot choose,
Because if you try, Christ you will lose.

Sin shall not have dominion over you I have read,
You must repent, that is what Christ said.
Even if you are living in sin Christ loves you still;
If His love you reject, death will be a bitter pill.

If in sin you choose to be,
Then only in judgment Jesus you will see,
So do you really wish to wait so long,
Until every opportunity has come and gone?

The price for my sins, I was unable to pay,
So in sin I must remain, there I must stay.
Then I heard Jesus came and died for my sins,
Now not for me only, but everyone wins.

No longer in sin will I walk,
And things about sin I no longer talk.
My life is now in Christ, that is what I choose to do,
Lord, it is You I serve, Lord I choose You.

I tried sin and it did not pay,
In sin satan wanted me to stay,
And in sin he wanted me to live every day,
But Jesus came and showed me a better way.

Haven't you had enough of sin?
Don't you want a new life to begin?
Christ is just waiting for you to say,
Lord, forgive me, I want that better way.

But if in sin you wish to remain,
And your old lifestyle you want to maintain,
Then with Christ you can never be,
Not returning to Christ and being set free.

Inspirational Poems of Encouragement

SOMEONE ALONG THE WAY

My life has sure had its share of pain.
And on my life sin has left its stain.
I thought a life in You would be a breeze.
And for once my life could be at ease.

When out in sin life was like a mighty storm.
Wearing away until I was battered and torn.
It has been a struggle just to survive.
But I now know why I am still alive.

Sin was keeping me on a well trodden path.
I was beginning to feel the results of its wrath.
And by my own doing it almost destroyed me.
You came or that is the way it would be.

With so much hurting it would have to show.
I got through this by a source I did not know.
I wanted something better but did not know what.
About God I had not heard a lot.

Lord long ago I wish You I would have known.
Then so many seeds of sin I would not have sown.
The way I was going, I know was the wrong way,
Now I am enjoying Your way better every day.

Is there anyone Lord I can talk to about You?
I am new and don't always know what to do.
But more about You I want to learn,
And the things of God I want to discern.

Just look to Me in the good times and bad.
I will give you a life like you never had.
I will have someone along the way you will meet.
Things that would destroy you, you will defeat.

Inspirational Poems of Encouragement

ONE DAY

One day the storms of life will all be past.
We will be home with Christ at last.
He has just been waiting for that day,
When He comes to catch us away.

One day our past we will remember no more.
Heaven has been waiting with an open door.
When the gates of pearl you pass through,
God is there waiting just for you.

One day there will be no more toils or pain;
Death will not be part of our lives again.
No more disappointments you had here,
No more heartache, not another tear.

One day those that have gone through so much,
Jesus will give you the final healing touch.
All the suffering you went through,
No more; a new body He has given you.

One day our sorrows and grief will be gone.
We are in Heaven, the place we waited for so long.
And we will leave this world without a "goodbye".
We wouldn't have time, anyway, for a reply.

One day all your troubles and trials will cease;
You have now entered the City of Peace.
You think you have gone through more than anyone else...
All these things have now passed — enjoy yourself!

One day we will reach that city with streets of gold,
Never again to walk streets slippery, freezing and cold.
But in that city where God has everything right,
Where it is eternal day, with no night.

Inspirational Poems of Encouragement

NO OTHER TIME LIKE THIS

The tribulation is just ahead,
And before it is over millions will be dead. Christ said,
"There will be no other time like this."
It will be everything but a time of bliss.

The ruler will come as a man of peace.
If possible, anything good he will cause to cease.
Very little peace will there be upon the earth,
And many will hate the day of their birth.

He will be given power he has never known,
Miracles he never did before will now be shown.
The world he will deceive,
And a mark he will cause them to receive.

There will be famine and distress throughout the land.
Many people will die. Death is on every hand.
There will be even more die later,
All because of this man, the God-hater.

There has never been anything like this before,
Misery and death will reign from shore to shore.
Jesus said, "We could escape this time of wrath,
But only if now we are on the right path."

Satan will rule the earth with an evil force,
On those that are not with Christ, of course.
He deceives the world with his flattering speech,
And tries to keep all he can from God's reach.

There will be no place for you to hide,
In Jesus, now is the place for us to abide.
There will be wrath on those that are still here.
You can't escape. It will be far and near.

In Jerusalem where this man will be,
The place where Jesus died and one day we will see.
He died there on the cross for you and me.
Make Him Lord now, and with Him you will forever be.

Inspirational Poems of Encouragement

WHAT HAPPENS NEXT?

A great event called the rapture is about to take place,
Then we will see the One that died for us--face to face.
There will be no time to repent,
Now after His body the Church, He has been sent.

We will be changed in the twinkling of an eye.
There will be no time to say goodbye.
No longer will these bodies be racked by pain;
We will have a new body, and with Him reign.

We will be caught up to meet Him in the air,
Those that are left can't say, "He was not fair."
Just ask Jesus to come and forgive you;
And this I know He will gladly do.

Is everything in order for you to go?
We might leave today or tomorrow, we do not know.
Those that die in the Lord will be raised from the dead.
That is His Word; that is what He said.

Are you so tired and weary you can't go on?
Hang on; I don't think it will be long.
Could His coming be tonight or morning or noon?
Could it really take place that soon?

Who can predict the time God has set?
Repent, Christ said, this command must be met.
His coming is certain, this I know,
If this command has been obeyed, you will go.

When the rapture takes place with God we will dwell.
It's not God's will that any perish and to go to hell.
If you ask Him, He will gladly forgive you today;
The life I found in Christ, I find to be the better way.

Inspirational Poems of Encouragement

EVER SINCE

Ever since that day I came to You,
I repented: that is what You said I must do.
That was such a wonderful day.
My life was changed; now I want it Your way.

Maybe during that time I did pout and fret,
But not one day I served You do I regret.
Ever since my life I gave to You,
It wasn't always smooth, but plenty of good times, too.

Ever since the day I made the decision to serve You,
I made up my mind to go all the way, too.
After all these years my mind is still the same:
Live for You and my life in You remain.

I have wondered why things turned out the way they did,
And why some things from me You kept hid.
But You always worked things out,
To bring good things about.

Of the time I have left on earth,
I worship the One that could make me of some worth.
Ever since the day I started this new walk,
My life changed, including my talk.

You know all the times I failed Thee.
There is no one I can blame but me.
Alone, You said, I would never be.
Looking back this fact I now can see.

I believe this life is almost finished.
My soul and spirit You kept replenished.
I'm glad my life with You I did commence:
The good life You gave, I've enjoyed…ever since.

Inspirational Poems of Encouragement

FROM THE PORTOLS OF HEAVEN

Christ looked down through the ages and He could see,
Without His death in sin I would forever be.
He could see the human race was going to hell;

It saddened Him to see how low man fell.
It grieved Him to see us in such a hopeless state.
I must die for them Father; He saw our fate.
If Adam had listened to what God had said,
No need for His blood to be shed.

He knew He would die, because of what Adam did.
This He must do, our sins He must rid.
How often have you wished your pain would go away?
If Adam had been faithful, you would not be in pain today.

Christ saw sin would enter the human race.
Adam had power to stand up for his rightful place.
But he failed, he gave in;
Now we must die, because of his sin.

Eve listened to the serpent and believed his lie.
Then her relationship with God began to die.
We now have the light; in it we must walk.
It is God we must listen to when He begins to talk.

When satan comes and causes you grief,
The things he speaks will never bring relief.
Satan's future has an end, it has been sealed.
The truth about his fate has now been revealed.

But for us there has come a brighter day,
Christ came to show us His way was the better way.
If to sin you are a slave,
Jesus will set you free, His life for you He willing gave.

Inspirational Poems of Encouragement

YOU AND ME

Jesus looked down and He could see,
He would have to come and die on that tree.
He did it willingly for you and me,
Or, with Him we could never be.

Once a sacrifice was a ram.
But for us, it was Christ the Lamb.
Oh, Lord, Your name is to be praised,
And what You do for us, I am so amazed.

So take courage, my friend,
The way things are now will come to an end.
We will forever with Jesus live,
Because, His life He did so freely give.

Who knows what tomorrow holds?
His revelation to us He gradually unfolds.
Sometimes He even lets us know what lies ahead,
Search His Word to find what He said.

There is no time to look back at the past,
Only those things in His Word will last.
Now in righteousness, everything we must do.
When temptations come, He will bring us through.

Can we comprehend what He went through;
The suffering and pain He had to do?
Because of our sins, He did it for me and you,
All that He went through.

There is much to look forward to;
Jesus will always be there for you.
Keep looking up, and one day you will see,
Jesus coming after you and me.

Inspirational Poems of Encouragement

I DID NOT QUIT

No longer do we walk alone,
His love to us He has shown.
One day with Jesus we will sit,
All because we did not quit.

If we are faithful, one day Jesus we shall see.
And by His grace, with Him we shall forever be.
With my praise I will give satan a fit.
And I will never quit.

What is there to go back to?
Without Jesus what good did we ever do?
Keep your eyes on the goal until you reach it,
And you will, because you did not quit.

Maybe there will be hard times ahead,
But don't forget, Jesus is not dead.
Do not let sin reign, not even a little bit.
Don't ever give in, don't ever quit.

Jesus said, "I will be there for you.
I will never leave you, I will see you through".
Jesus, to You my life I fully commit.
It is no problem now to say, I will not quit.

Do you know Jesus? He will set you free.
He will gladly do it, as He did for me.
Try Him if only for a little bit.
Then I know you will say; I will never quit.

Jesus will always be by your side.
That river you cross might be deep and wide,
But His love and mercy there is plenty of it.
Then you as I can say, "I did not quit."

Now God is awaiting me,
Because of His Son who died on that tree.
Now in His kingdom I do so wondrously fit,
All because I did not quit.

Inspirational Poems of Encouragement

TIME OUT PRAY

Is there just a few minutes you could give and pray?
God loves to hear from you every day.
It is easy to pray while on your way,
But take a little of your own time and pray.

Is praying such a chore for you to do?
Jesus took time out of His busy life for you.
Spare a few minutes of time in prayer to Him?
In prayer, it keeps our light from growing dim.

There is so little time in a day, but so much to do.
Just ask Him; He will make a little time for you.
Then you can go into your closet and pray.
I believe you will have a better day.

Do you have time on the weekends to play?
Take just a few minutes of that time to pray?
He will listen to what you have to say,
Because you took of your own time to pray.

I, myself, know the hustle and bustle of living.
We must also take a little time for giving.
The Lord knows what you have to do; He will help you,
But He wants a little of your time, too.

Lord, forgive me for not taking more time for You.
You did so much for me, things I could never do.
I must take the time to pray, this I know
And find the time; to me You will show.

He took time out of His life to die for you;
He did for you what no one else could do.
So take a few minutes for Him and say,
I will take a few minutes now, and pray.

Inspirational Poems of Encouragement

IT JUST WAITS ON GOD

The dandelion is a nuisance. It is a pain.
Yet God supplies it with sun and rain.
But for me You died! Now I am alive.
Lord, without You, neither of us could survive.

It would be easy for it to quit when things go wrong,
But if it had, long ago it would be gone.
All its troubles God brings it through.
He does far more for me and you.

Step on it. Crush it. Run over it with the mower,
It will come back as if seeds were sown by the sower.
Don't let every little thing knock me off my feet,
Because each day with God I meet.

How can we give up, when God loves us so?
The dandelion doesn't, and God it does not know.
It does not beg or plead.
It just waits on God for its need.

God gives both of us endurance.
He gave me eternal life; I have His assurance.
I am in Christ, my roots go deep.
He put me in His harvest, I must reap.

The dandelion is a pest,
Yet every day it gives God its best.
Can I say the same for man?
Through Christ, our tribulations we can overcome, we can.

The dandelion is hardy and strong.
It does not grow weary when things go wrong.
What can I learn from that little weed?
That God will supply my every need.

The dandelion is a survivor and so am I.
We both wait on God that is why.
It never says times are hard, I am going to quit.
Neither will I until that day with God I sit.

Inspirational Poems of Encouragement

THE TONGUE

The tongue is such a tiny member;
Let me tell you something you need to remember.
In a short time it can cause so much destruction,
It might take a lifetime of reconstruction.

That tiny member is the hardest to tame.
On it much of life's troubles we can blame.
Against a good person it can cause so much pain,
Their life might never get back together again.

Small as it may be, it has caused so much harm,
And by its smooth words can spread its charm.
It doesn't mind who it hurts along the way,
As long as it has the last say.

It has spread its lies and deceit,
And has gotten good, these things it will repeat.
It has said things about its best friend.
Its destruction never seems to end.

It doesn't mind on whom it tells a lie,
And the good character of a man must die.
On and on the vicious cycle goes,
How many people it has hurt, only Jesus knows.

What it says sometimes can be very brief,
But can cause a lifetime of grief.
Are you going to let it have the last word?
It can cause you to miss Heaven; you must be assured.

Turn your life over to Jesus now.
He can even change the tongue; He knows just how.
Don't let it any longer control your life.
It has already caused enough pain and strife.

Inspirational Poems of Encouragement

WHEN I NEED YOU

How long, Lord, since my burdens You helped bear?
How long since any time with me You did spare?
Once grace did abound,
Now when I need You most, You can't be found.

Don't You see my troubles and my fears?
Can't You see all this pain and my tears?
How much longer, Lord, must I wait?
You know sin I also hate.

I wish I was dreaming and this would go away,
But You don't come, and it continues day after day.
If I could, I would take care of these things.
So much was between us; now so little remains.

I find myself in such a plight,
When I need You, You take Your flight.
I wish there was something You would do.
Come Lord, won't You?

Is there more on the way?
Is there something You will do today?
I sure wish I knew.
If there is more what will I do?

Why must the problems always stay?
From things that grieve You, I have stayed away.
You said for us to ask.
Then why is getting an answer such a task?

I know you have served Me from your youth,
And you have held on to the truth.
The answer you are looking for is just ahead.
I know what you have wished for and said.

Inspirational Poems of Encouragement

A PRAYER FOR THE HURTING

Father, I pray for all those that are hurting today,
That their hurts would not continue, but soon go away.
I don't know all the things they are going through,
But You do.

I don't know what many are having to face today;
A husband, a wife that has gone astray.
If only they would return to the One that says, "I am the way",
To the One that still solves problems today.

Father, many need an answer for their life,
It is filled with misery, toils and strife.
We pray for the widows with their struggles, all alone,
Come visit them and let your presence be shown.

Parents who have children on drugs, who have run away,
I pray they would soon return maybe today.
These hurts and sorrows are not hidden from You,
You have the answer, You know what to do.

Many have hurts that never occurred in my life,
The aches, the pains, and friends that cause strife.
We pray for the parents, who are on alcohol and drugs,
Children whose mom and dad are not giving them hugs.

Lord, You see those marriages that are unfaithful,
Those that have a good wife or husband but are ungrateful.
Lord we pray for the marriages that are falling apart,
I pray they would find a new start.

Lord I pray for the children that are being used,
Things that were never meant to be; they are being abused.
And for the elderly, Lord, I pray,
That as long as possible at home they might stay.

Jesus knows all the hurts you are going through;
I know personally He will be there for you.
Jesus loves you and He cares.
Your sorrows, your heartaches He shares.

Inspirational Poems of Encouragement

THROW IN THE TOWEL

Are you angry and ready to throw in the towel?
And at God you are ready to scream foul?
You thought God would always be there.
But if He was, you were unaware.

You don't get an answer when you pray,
Even when you pray day after day.
He no longer cares and you're ready to quit,
Things keep going from bad to worse bit by bit.

Does there seem to be no hope?
You think; can one more day I cope?
There is certainly nothing to look forward to,
And with God you think you are through.

You know your tomorrows will be as bad as today,
Because your tomorrows turn out the same ole way.
And you think you had just as soon be dead.
Since God you can't find, and alone you must tread.

Do you wish the days ahead would be brighter,
And your burdens would be lighter?
Are you walking down a path and going nowhere?
Is God still with me? I am not sure.

If I cast You aside, I could see why this would be,
You don't seem interested; it seems to me.
My life was like a flower in bloom;
Now gladness of Spirit is gone, it is only gloom.

Keep looking up, Jesus has always been there.
God promises He is with you even if you are unaware.
He sees and understands your every care.
Don't give up; soon eternal life with Jesus you will share.

Inspirational Poems of Encouragement

YOU CHANGED MY LIFE

Lord, to You my life I freely give,
My life through You I want to live.
Long ago on that special day,
My life I gave in forty nine in the month of May.

I will never forget that day I came to You.
You forgave me; it was what You wanted to do.
All because on a cross for me You died,
Now I have You on my side.

Jesus, You came and suffered so much pain.
If You hadn't, in sin I would remain.
Now, no longer do I walk in sin,
I have Christ in my heart, He now dwells within.

I'm sorry You had to die, but willing to do,
Now I can live my new life through You.
You changed my life from darkness to light,
Now my world is shining bright.

If You had said no and not come to this earth,
I would not know of the new birth.
There would be nothing I could do but perish,
And never see the one I love and most cherish.

Lord, mold me that I might be more like Thee,
Fulfilling the mission You gave to me,
Without You there would not be one poem to write,
To tell others Jesus loves them, He is the light.

Lord, all that I am or ever will be is because of You,
In troubles, in sorrows, You brought me through,
Now Lord since my life belongs to You,
I want to finish the work You gave me to do.

Inspirational Poems of Encouragement

WHEN I GET OLD

Lord, never let me get old, so no more I can do.
Doing all I can for Your kingdom, too.
I remember the day You came into my life to live,
But first my sins You had to forgive.

It has been many years since that day,
Since You changed my life and moved in to stay.
I wouldn't trade my walk with You for anything.
My heart rejoices and there's still a song to sing.

When I get old will You give me poems to write?
I never want to be idle, but fighting the fight.
I know people older than me.
They are busy for You; that's the way I want it to be.

Getting old I never thought I would do,
But by now be home with You.
I know there will always be something to do.
Will each day bring something new?

When I get old I can still pray,
Always close to You I want to stay.
The Holy Spirit I never want to grieve,
But at all times be ready to leave.

Lord, I need wisdom for each day,
To know what to do and say.
Always keeping in sight my goal,
I will stand before God, perfect and whole.

I wish I would have done more while getting old,
Listening and doing what I was told.
I want to be doing Your will, when I get old,
Or, until I walk with You down those streets of gold.

Inspirational Poems of Encouragement

I CAN ONLY IMAGINE

I can only imagine what it will be like when I see Your face,
In times of trouble You supplied me with grace.
I can only imagine the love You have for me,
I will only know when with You I will be.

I can only imagine what You suffered for me,
But You knew it was the way it had to be.
I can only imagine if You had not come,
I would die in my sins, that is the sum.

I can only imagine what it would be without Your Word,
Am I on my way to Heaven? I could not be assured.
I can only imagine what life would be without You,
I would not know the One that is true.

I can only imagine when You created the universe,
Or on earth one day there would be a curse.
I can only imagine the discussion of Your coming to die,
And then in someone else's tomb You would lie.

I can only imagine how the planets were hung,
Some say the earth is old, some say relatively young.
I can only imagine how old You are,
Or to Heaven, is it far?

I can only imagine when there was only the three of You,
What was on Your mind, what did You do?
Then came the creation and oh, how vast,
From Your fingertips the planets were cast.

I can only imagine the way Heaven must be,
Maybe soon I will get to see,
I can only imagine what in Heaven You have for me,
But I will know, because You died on that tree.

Inspirational Poems of Encouragement

HEAVEN OF BRASS

To brass Heaven must have turned.
I have sought You, after You I have yearned.
Why Lord do I have this feeling,
My prayer is getting no higher than the ceiling?

Does Heaven have to be this way?
Is it going to be of brass again today?
Will tomorrow be the same?
Heaven turns to brass at the mention of Your name.

Can't just once be a get-through day?
Or does Heaven turn to brass only when I pray?
Must my prayers on earth remain?
Won't there ever be an answer again?

Nowhere do my prayers seem to go.
Why Heaven stays of brass, I do not know.
When I call, why have You not heard?
I know You hear, it is written in Your Word.

Lord, turn Heaven back to normal for me,
Or, is this the way it is always going to be?
Is there anything more I must do
Before my prayer gets through to You?

I never thought it would be this way.
Won't You listen; won't You hear today?
Why even bother anymore to pray,
If brass is the way Heaven is going to stay.

You say I'm not listening, I have not heard.
I have been listening, I heard every word.
Do not be discouraged when you pray.
The answer now could be on the way.

Inspirational Poems of Encouragement

IN CONTROL

Lord, over all the earth You are in control,
And the angels You send to patrol.
Nothing is missed by You; You see all,
Even the sparrow when to the ground it does fall.

So who is keeping anything from You hid?
We read of all the things You did.
So why are we so secret about the things we do,
When all the time You already knew?

You created the heavens and the wide-open spaces.
You see the smiles or hurts upon our faces.
You created the earth and sea,
And just for Yourself, You created me.

Lord, I am glad You are Who You are.
You told of the new birth and we are better off by far.
Only You know what lies ahead.
In place of sin and death, You gave us life instead.

I am glad the earth is in Your hands.
You know each person by name in all lands.
So who better to commit all our troubles to?
You have everything in control and know what to do.

Lord, for the good of all You will work things out.
Looking after us is what You are all about.
With so much turmoil, strife and pain,
Only You can put broken lives back together again.

Lord, I am glad the earth is still controlled by You,
And will be even when it is made anew.
You are just waiting for weary souls to come to You.
You give them hope; this You want so much to do.

Inspirational Poems of Encouragement

THE CROSS

Jesus died on the cross for our sins that day.
He knew there was no other way.
Heaven had a temporary loss;
While Jesus came and died on the cross.

"The cross is not a good way to die, I know.
But for the people we created, I will go.
Going to the cross is what I must do.
I must get the family back for You."

Jesus took the curse when He died on that tree.
No one else could do that for me.
Dying was what He came to do,
And the cross was the way, He knew.

The cross, there was a need for one.
On it must die, God's Son.
Death on the cross is the way it had to be.
No other way could it be done for me.

It was said, "Christ must be lifted up".
The cross was that bitter cup.
No more need for the cross will there ever be.
Once was enough for all eternity.

It was Heaven and earth's gain, not loss,
When Jesus died on the cross.
He came to show us the way.
It was now time to die; this was the day.

What will you do with Jesus that died on the cross?
It can be your gain or loss.
The decision, at some time, will have to be made.
The price for your sins, Jesus paid.

Inspirational Poems of Encouragement

WILDEST DREAM

The sacrifice that was offered long ago is good today.
His blood was shed to wash our sins away.
Why did you choose sin when you knew what to do?
You couldn't use the excuse, I never heard of You.

He has been waiting to hear from you.
Just let Him do for you what He wants to do.
He will give you a life beyond your wildest dream.
The two of you would sure make a team.

What a change; even those you hate you can love.
That love is from God above.
Your life He will completely rearrange.
Your old friends will quickly see the change.

Today He would like to turn your life around,
Because by sin you are bound.
A much better life He wants to give.
Only then can you truly say I live.

The sacrifice that was offered long ago,
His love and mercy to you He wants to show.
You can be set free from sin
When you ask Jesus to come to dwell within.

Until I asked Jesus to forgive me all was not well.
His Word told me I was on my way to hell.
He was patient just waiting on me.
He must see something in me I was unable to see.

Now He is waiting patiently for you to say,
Change my life; I want it to be a better way.
Oh how quickly He will reply.
He came to give hope, but first He must die.

Inspirational Poems of Encouragement

HEAVEN

I want to finish the work the Lord gave me.
But in Heaven is where I want to be,
Because Jesus I long to see
The One that came and died for me.

About Heaven I have heard.
And read about streets of gold in His Word,
With gates of pearl at the entrance to each street.
Jesus will take me there, and in the air we will meet.

God is preparing a place there for me.
He loves me that is the way He wants it to be.
I read of Abraham, Isaac and Jacob who are there.
And that Heaven is a place God wants to share.

Surely Heaven is a place all would want to go.
But by their lives and deeds it does not show.
Heaven is more beautiful than our valleys and hills.
There is no sickness, no need for money, no more bills.

Are you prepared to go to that Heavenly place?
Or will you one day face Him in disgrace?
Heaven is a place God has prepared for all.
If you listen I know you will hear Him call.

So come, come go with me.
Make Jesus Lord, if Him you want to see.
An invitation He has also given you,
Because He wants you to be there, too.

Only a little about Heaven in His Word we are told.
But on what I have read and heard I am sold.
There is only one way for sure for me to know.
Check on it myself....Go....

Inspirational Poems of Encouragement

IN HIM WE NOW ABIDE

Long ago, Jesus came and died;
Of this fact the prophets testified.
Because of sin, Heaven we would miss.
Jesus came and did something about this.

God saw the plight we were in.
Jesus, alone, could rid us of sin.
So He came and was our guide.
Then He died.

The price for sin, I could not pay.
So Christ came; He was the way.
The things about Jesus, God's Word verified.
Then He died.

Man had lost his way.
To redeem him, there was a price to pay.
"It is finished!" Jesus cried.
Then He died.

In His Word we are told,
The price of a slave, He was sold.
God's Word, from us, He did not hide.
Then He died.

A sacrifice was required since the fall.
The sacrifice Jesus made is good for all.
Jesus preached, raised the dead, and was crucified.
Then He died.

God saw He would have to give His Son.
No one else would do; He was the only One.
In Him we now abide,
Because Jesus died.

Inspirational Poems of Encouragement

MORE LIKE THEE

Lord, just make me more like You.
In everything I think about and do.
My own way I don't want it to be,
But to be more like Thee.

I know at times You I grieve.
You never say, I am going to leave,
But when I ask, You always forgive me.
I want to be more like Thee.

Your love shows in everything You do;
That is why I want to pattern my life after You.
When I falter You still love me;
That is why I want to be more like Thee.

If we go astray You are still so forgiving;
That is why serving You makes life worth living.
Make whatever changes in me there needs to be,
So I will be more like Thee.

For me You went more than the second mile.
You died for me and on my face placed a smile.
One day You gave Your very best for me;
That is why I want to be more like Thee.

Lord when I vary and get off track,
You are there waiting to welcome me back.
Whatever You expect of me, this I want to be.
I just want to be more like Thee.

Life with You I know is awaiting me,
Because of Your death upon that tree.
A body that won't grow old You have for me;
Then I will even be more like Thee.

Inspirational Poems of Encouragement

GOD'S WORD SAYS

Let God's Word always have a place in your heart.
Study It so in your life It will be a part.
It will guide you when everything else fails.
It will keep you when the storms of life assail.

Do you still worry and fret?
Are you the better for it yet?
Turn to God's Word; it has stood the test
And will show you how to get His best.

Satan is sure to follow you around.
He will be on your heels like a hound
And you might not know what to do.
God's Word says, "I will always be there for you".

When everything goes wrong in your life,
God's Word will keep you from bitterness and strife.
When satan comes at you with all he's got,
Remember God's grace. He has a lot.

Does it seem God is so far away;
There is no reason any longer to pray?
God's Word says He is always near;
There is no need to fear.

When satan tells you God does not care,
He is not listening, He does not hear,
You won't find Him no matter how hard you try.
God's Word says His ears are open to your cry.

You think your burdens are more than you can bear.
Life has you beaten down; it just isn't fair.
You will never have to walk life's path alone.
God is still God and has never lost His throne.

Inspirational Poems of Encouragement

IN THE HOLLOW OF MY HAND

Is there a reason to go on?
You have forsaken me; You are gone.
Is there a cause for this to be?
Why have You forgotten me?

What is the purpose any more, to try?
It doesn't seem to matter if I live or die.
I have called and You did not hear?
I asked and You did not draw near.

I was hoping You had come at last.
But once again, by me You must have passed.
To serve You, I made up my mind to do.
Now where are You?

How much more can I take?
I have searched for You when awake.
Lord, I have tried to give You my best.
Why, now, are you taking Your rest?

Your presence I can no longer feel.
My spirit You do not come and heal.
Can I get through one more day?
Why do You no longer come my way?

Life has been like struggling through mire.
I get so weary; I surely do tire.
Why does life have to be like this?
Death would be a joy; life I would not miss.

"Your struggles, all about them, I know.
Revelation to you I now show.
For Me, you have made your stand.
All the time, I kept you in the hollow of My hand!"

Inspirational Poems of Encouragement

GOD'S MERCY

Sin and mercy started in the garden;
Only God could show mercy, and give a pardon.
There was no place they could hide;
No longer did God walk by their side.

Sin became part of the life of Adam, Eve, and Cain,
And in every person sin would reign
Until the time when Jesus came,
Now mercy and forgiveness we did regain.

When it was time for the flood,
Noah offered a sacrifice of blood.
It was a type of sacrifice that would be revealed,
The sins of all mankind could be healed.

God shows his mercy to a thousand generations,
And reveals His mercy and manifestations.
Mercy is shown to the strong and the weak;
It is given if we follow Him and mercies seek.

At the cross God's mercy to us was shown.
Man didn't deserve God's will to be known.
His mercy is shown to us all;
Won't you listen to Him now, and heed His call?

Just come to Jesus, He will show His mercy now.
Jesus will help you, He knows just how.
If only you knew how much He loves you,
If you knew how much for you He wants to do.

On the cross mercy was shown to all that day.
But to reveal His mercy, a great price He must pay.
But until the time our goal we reach,
Jesus, love, and mercy we must teach.

Inspirational Poems of Encouragement

THIS PAIN

Has life dealt you a bitter blow?
God, where are You? I just don't seem to know.
Don't You see my struggles, don't You see my pain?
I need a downpour of Spiritual rain.

If only I knew these troubles would go away.
Is this pain going to stay?
Lord, is Heaven closed to my pain and struggles?
Won't You come in times of my troubles?

Lord, almost daily I pray and get into Your Word,
Why has it been so long since I have heard?
In all this misery must I remain?
You know from evil I continued to refrain.

My problems just seem to never go away.
They just keep coming day after day.
So Lord, when will I hear from You?
You always knew just what to do.

Lord, it seems, at least in the past,
This pain did not always last.
But now it seems it is here to stay;
Won't You come now, won't You come today?

While on earth I went through much pain,
God brought Me through, for you He will do the same.
I know exactly what you are going through,
I am still your friend; I will be there for you.

I hear each time you pray;
I have not gone away.
Your day is coming, you will see,
The sun will rise again; with you I will always be.

Inspirational Poems of Encouragement

I REMEMBER

The day I asked Christ into my life I remember very well.
To make a change, I needed Him to come in and dwell.
Sin I wanted out of my life, of it I am now rid.
Who did this for me? Jesus did.

Sin in my life only Christ could remove.
And only You, my life could improve.
No longer to sin do I have to bow;
Christ came, He dwells there now.

Sin in my life once did dwell.
Christ delivered me, so you, I now can tell.
I am no longer in bondage to sin.
Christ took that away; now He lives within.

All I could see was sin and death in me.
Was there something else in me Christ could see?
Did He see one day Him I would serve?
I called: and a place in Heaven You did reserve.

Not one of Your creation do You want to perish.
You love each one; each one You cherish.
The price for sin has been paid;
The foundation for righteousness has been laid.

His love reaches out to all that will come.
Buy milk and honey without cost; it is free to everyone.
Only God knew one day what would take place,
He prepared a sacrifice for me or death I would face.

If you are tired of the way you live,
Christ is the answer: your life to Him give.
He will hear if you ask, so ask, be the next one.
He is waiting with arms outstretched….come.

Inspirational Poems of Encouragement

WHEN GOD TAKES A LOOK

The Book of Life is the name of this book.
Will your name be there when God takes a look?
I repented and my sins, from me, God took.
That's how I got my name in the book.

His Son, to the earth, was sent.
Now God requires all to repent.
Repent, if you want your name in the book.
Will God see it when He takes a look?

Jesus said, "I am the Way."
So invite Him into your life today.
It's the way your name can be added in the book.
Will God see it when it comes time to take a look?

Sin in Heaven can never be.
That is why I ask Him to forgive me.
I know my name is written in the book
And God will see it when it comes time to take a look.

Will yours be there when God calls your name?
There will be no one else you can blame.
God is waiting to add your name in the book.
Will He find it when it comes time to take a look?

Don't put off coming to Christ another day.
You will be glad you found this glorious way!
The angels rejoice when your name is put in the book.
You will also rejoice when God takes a look.

On Judgment Day, will your name be in the book?
It is for certain God will look.
It will be if sin you forsook.
God wants it there when He takes a look.

Inspirational Poems of Encouragement

ON THE ROAD TO HELL

Without You, Lord, there would be no song,
And everything that could would go wrong.
If You had not died for me,
On the road to hell I would be.

If You had not come and Your love shown,
The Truth, I never would have known.
If You had not died on that tree,
On the road to hell I would be.

If You had not come and died,
There would be no Word to rightly divide.
If You did not care about me,
On the road to hell I would be.

If You had not come to this earth,
I would not know of the new birth.
What then would happen to me?
On the road to hell I would be.

If You had not come to die,
No need to seek You, no need to try.
What would become of me?
On the road to hell I would be.

If You had not come and died,
In You I could never abide.
There would be no hope for me.
On the road to hell I would be.

"From the beginning I knew what I would do.
I knew I would have to die for you.
There was no one else God could send but Me.
No longer on the road to hell, do you have to be.

Inspirational Poems of Encouragement

A CONVERSATION IN HEAVEN

A conversation took place in Heaven long ago.
Who can I send to earth? Who will go?
A mission there I have in mind.
The people are not always loving and kind.

They will put a crown of thorns on Your head.
They will rejoice when You are dead.
It will take love for them when You go.
They will be cruel to You, I know.

The One that goes will be spit upon.
The people there will treat You wrong.
They will slap You on the face.
And try to disgrace.

You have never known such pain.
You must die but I will raise You up again.
It will be a great sacrifice to go there.
Their sins, on a cross, You must bear.

This is not a pleasure trip.
Your garments from You, they will strip.
To the people on earth, You must preach the Word.
Then send them until everyone has heard.

Nothing short of death will do.
And everything will depend on You.
You will suffer humiliation and shame,
For their wrongs, You must bear the blame.

The people there will hang You on a tree.
Now who will go and that sacrifice be?
So Jesus came and died and suffered all that pain;
The price it took for us to be born again.

Inspirational Poems of Encouragement

ALL ALONE

Has life bounced you around like a ball?
And each time harder seems to be the fall?
You wish some way this would be finished.
And your weary soul replenished.

Why does this continue on this way?
Will I be able to take this one more day?
Through life alone must I go?
Everything about me You know.

For me it seems to always be an uphill go.
And what tomorrow holds I do not know.
Lord, why from me are you staying hid?
Reveal to me if anything against You I did.

Why are You always so far away?
Or, are You just too busy to come when I pray?
I was hoping soon there would be a break.
But it seems my own way I have to take.

I thought You were a God who cared.
And all my troubles with You could be shared.
But if I have to wait too long,
Will I have the strength to press on?

Does it not matter to You the way I feel?
You do not come to touch me and heal?
Is all my life going to be this way?
In this condition must I always stay?

You thought you were facing all this alone.
And you think My love was not shown.
Since your conception I was with you all the time.
And will be until the day you are sublime.

Inspirational Poems of Encouragement

HAVE YOU FORGOTTEN ME?

Lord, why have You turned Your back on me?
The things I am going through, don't You see?
I know You love me, because You suffered and died.
The things I've been through, are You not satisfied?

You said we wouldn't face these battles alone.
Is there something in my life You want to hone?
When will there be a little relief?
Is peace gone, and nothing left but pain and grief?

Why don't You answer when Your name I call upon?
Have You forgotten me; will You answer before long?
Are things between us not the same?
If I have done wrong, I will take the blame.

From me You must have taken Your flight
In my heart I believe I am doing what is right.
You have just vanished from sight.
Must my days also be turned into night?

Lord, it seems I am just worn out.
Is this what serving You is all about?
If it would help, out loud would I shout.
Would You just put me on a different route?

Even in the worst of times after You I did seek.
Won't You look down; won't You take a peek?
Don't You see how badly I hurt?
Then me also You desert.

Do you know someone whose world has turned upside down?
And they feel they have been trampled right into the ground?
Go and encourage them, and for them pray.
And I truly believe your own troubles will start to vanish away.

Inspirational Poems of Encouragement

DRINK FROM HIS FOUNTAIN

Your life has been a real mess.
And your sins you would not confess.
God wanted to give you a life filled with good.
If only He could.

Without Him is your life fulfilled?
On a cross for you His blood was spilled.
He fulfilled all about Him that were written.
That is why He was smitten.

He saw how low in sin we were.
He would have to die; this He knew for sure.
Why did He go through so much pain?
To have our relationship with God back again.

Your godly parents can't help on judgment day.
For your own sins you will have to pay.
Christ has taken care of that for you; die, He must do.
You must repent; that is what He requires of you.

If you want to join Him where He dwells,
Come, drink from His fountain and His deep wells.
There has been no greater love ever shown.
Christ came and made salvation known.

His love for you that day was so great.
He fulfilled His mission to save you from your awful fate.
He asks you to come just as you are.
The door to salvation He will not bar.

The sacrifice for our sins is now complete.
Each year He need not repeat.
He died on the cross the scriptures say,
For you to have life; it was the only way

Inspirational Poems of Encouragement

YOU JUST DON'T CARE

Lord why do You no longer care?
Why my burdens alone must I bear?
My life with You I always planned to share.
Now, You just don't care.

We used to have so many good talks.
And together we took our walks.
The path I was on seemed so clear.
Now, You just don't care.

My life was filled with joy and peace.
Lord what happened that caused it to cease?
You used to hold me dear.
Now, You just don't care.

There was a time I know You loved me.
Now my troubles You no longer see.
When I call You do not hear.
Because, You just don't care.

Our relationship used to be so good.
I thought coming to you I always could.
You used to be so near.
Now, You just don't care.

Must I cry out to You night and day?
You turn Your head and look the other way?
Why has my life turned from joy to fear?
Because, You just don't care.

If I didn't care I would have stayed with the Father.
If I didn't care, to die why would I even bother?
Alone you would face your troubles and fear.
You have never been alone, and yes, I do care.

Inspirational Poems of Encouragement

NEED A TOUCH

Lord, when I should feel good, why do I feel so rotten?
When I need You the most, why am I forgotten?
It was You that said I am the Lord that healeth thee.
Yet, when I call upon You, there seems no time for me.

With all this pain I sure need a touch.
Won't You come; I need it so much.
This is something You should understand.
Yet You never touch me with Your healing hand.

You know I love You so much.
Now where are You when I so badly need a touch?
It feels like on me the whole world has come to batter.
And You don't seem to care; it just doesn't matter.

Lord, You know when this suffering began,
I cried out to You time and again.
But You weren't there for me.
Why is it my suffering You cannot see?

I didn't know anyone could suffer this bad.
I seem to have lost the joy and peace I once had.
Surely, Lord, about all this suffering You know.
Why then do You not come when I need You so?

Are You going to continue to pass me by?
When I call why do You not reply?
What good is it doing to seek and get into Your Word?
Because when I pray my voice is not heard.

I created the worlds, I created you.
Suffering and shame I also went through.
You will once again rejoice and be glad.
You will think it is the greatest day you ever had.

Inspirational Poems of Encouragement

SERVANT

I came to You, Lord, when but a teen.
Sin in my life You removed and made me clean.
One day I called upon Your name,
And that day Your servant I became.

Lord, I want to be a faithful servant,
In everything I do being fervent.
A great servant I may never be,
But fulfilling the call You have given me.

If You speak, I want to hear,
To help others, showing I care.
Make me that servant that will obey,
Always being prayed up and ready for the day.

I know there is plenty yet to do,
A humble servant I want to be for You.
Serving You with all my heart,
And be renewed, as each new day with You I start.

Even the King of Glory came to serve,
Or we would be doomed and get what we deserve.
Make me the best servant I can be,
So you can accomplish what You want in me.

I don't worry about what You give others to do,
As long as I am trusting and serving You.
To do what is right is expected of me,
Or a good servant I could not be.

Lord, help me to do my best,
That I have been faithful and stood the test.
And, You will say, "A good servant you have been;
And a new life with Me you can begin."

Inspirational Poems of Encouragement

THAT BRIGHT AND MORNING STAR

Lord, You are that bright and morning star.
How I wish I could be where You are.
But for now, I must remain where I am
Thank You for becoming my sacrificial lamb.

In this world of doom and gloom,
We can have peace, if for Christ we have made room.
You came to this earth at the time appointed,
And preached the gospel; You are God's anointed.

Why would You come to the earth?
Take on the form of man and have a human birth.
Could it be You loved the people of this land?
The people You created by Your own hand?

There are things I might never know;
Why to the cross, You would go.
Only by Your death could we live,
And only when we repent, can You forgive.

In this world of so much greed,
Your love and Spirit is what we need.
So Your love, through us, can be shown,
And Your name, to all people, be known.

How could You love us so much?
We didn't deserve Your loving touch.
We had all gone astray.
That is why You came and died that day.

You have always been the same.
You chose us to bear Your name.
You died for all, that's the way it had to be;
If I was the only one, You would have died for me.

Inspirational Poems of Encouragement

THE SACRIFICE

No other sacrifice would do.
God sent His Son to die for me and you.
"Let this cup pass from Me", Jesus cried.
It wasn't enough though, until He died.

On the cross Jesus cried.
He has suffered enough, so He died.
Now God was fully satisfied;
Never again would He be tested and tried.

Now we come to God, in Jesus' Name,
The One that was and will always be the same.
How would I have ever known the way
If Jesus had not come and died that day?

God thought His plan out very well.
Without His Son's death, I would go to hell.
Jesus did come to show me the way.
Then the time came and He died that day.

Many years have come and gone,
And things are certain to go wrong.
Satan sees to it that it happens that way,
But the sacrifice was sufficient for me that day.

Now, no other sacrifice is needed.
My life according to His Word I have heeded.
His Word now always shows me His way;
All because He sacrificed His life for me that day.

So now the only sacrifice I ask of you
Is to give your life to Me and I will show you what to do.
And I will keep you as you go down life's pathway,
As I listened to My Father and died for you that day.

Inspirational Poems of Encouragement

DO WHAT'S RIGHT

Lord, the best things in life I have missed.
"Do what's right," friends would insist.
Why didn't I listen to what they had to say?
I would know so much more about God today.

If only I could live my life over again.
Then a much different life I would begin.
If I could turn back time on my life I would.
My life to Christ I would give; if only I could.

No one knows this better than me.
Sin does not pay, on this I have to agree.
No one is more qualified than me to say;
Far away from sin you must stay.

The path I was on I was going the wrong way.
But the right decision I finally made one day.
When God opened my eyes so I could see,
Where the path I was on was leading me.

So many mistakes along the way I made,
And for them I have surely paid.
But God was merciful and forgave me.
This is the way He always wanted it to be.

Let me tell you a little about sin.
It is a deceiver; you can never win.
But if you decide to change your ways,
Christ gives a better life than all your yesterdays.

One more bit of advice I have for you.
Give your life to Christ; that do.
Then you won't face your guilt and shame,
But be free of the things you are to blame.

Inspirational Poems of Encouragement

REPENT

The way to eternal life Jesus came to show,
Now He wants the whole world to know;
In sin man did live,
So Your life You had to give.

What was right I did not do,
You still loved me and died for me, too.
You saw the terrible state I was in,
Because of my life of sin.

No one else for my sins could I blame,
Our sins caused You to suffer shame.
Because of sin You came and died;
It was a cruel death…crucified.

You knew death You must face,
It was the only way to redeem the human race.
A little time on earth You spent,
And preached, "you must repent".

"Repent and believe the gospel," 1 Jesus said;
Heaven and hell, your choice, both are just ahead.
I'm glad I finally heeded Your call;
We must repent one and all.

If in Heaven one day you want to be,
You must repent and from sin be set free.
To hell you do not have to go,
Jesus came and told us so.

Is Christ's death going to be in vain?
It will if you are not born again.
But if you repent, Christ will gladly forgive;
A new life in Him you will begin to live.

Inspirational Poems of Encouragement

HE HAS RISEN

He came out of the grave; He rose today.
We now can rejoice, sing and pray,
Until that day when He calls us away.
This could be the day.

But until that glorious day,
We must work, fast and pray.
When Jesus comes for us, He will feel proud.
He will tell the trumpeter to make it loud.

What we have longed for will become a reality,
When we put on immortality.
There will be no more death and pain.
We will live again.

The grave cannot hold us there.
No more burdens to bear.
That day will end all our sorrows,
And begin so many wonderful tomorrows.

He will be coming after you and me,
And with Him we will forever be.
Then this old body will be new.
There will be no limit to what we can do.

He is alive, I proclaim.
A resurrected body Jesus has and we will have the same.
Soon we will be with Him,
A brand new life we will begin.

We were once held in prison,
Now set free because Christ has risen.
"Death could not hold Him", God's Word did say.
He's alive! Yes, He rose today.

Inspirational Poems of Encouragement

HIS COMING

I am now getting older and gray.
Not much longer on earth do I plan to stay.
I believe His coming could be most any day;
Then Christ will catch us away.

Each day we go our way,
Not knowing what God's plan is for us today;
But if we listen He will tell,
When we know all will be well.

Of His coming I would not dare to guess,
But He needs to soon to straighten out this mess.
When He has planned to come, I do not know;
Occupy until you hear the trumpet blow.

His coming I have waited so long to see,
A part of it I know I will be;
Oh, what a home going day.
Welcome home, I am waiting to hear Him say.

Could there be a little while yet to wait?
Can we win one more before it is too late?
We must tell everyone the good news;
Every moment left we must wisely use.

His coming will be a time to rejoice,
What joy when we hear His voice.
Come up here we want to hear Him say,
This is the day.

Whenever the coming of the Lord is,
We will have a new body like His.
What a glorious change that will be,
And Jesus we will finally see.

Inspirational Poems of Encouragement

NEVER PASS AWAY

Thank You, Lord, for doing for us what You did
And not keeping God's Word from us hid,
But revealing to us what God has to say:
The price for our sins You had to pay.

Your Word is not for just a special few.
In it you can find something refreshing and new.
It tells about salvation, grace, and healing,
And each day becomes more revealing.

There has nothing been like it before.
That is why at the proper time You let us know.
For such a long time You had this in mind.
Now it was time to reveal it to all mankind.

Your Word has yet to be destroyed by man.
He has tried; he still thinks he can.
God's Word will always be around,
In it your destiny can be found.

So many things in His Word there are to learn.
But with many it is not a concern.
God has all these good things for me and you.
Go tell your friends, neighbors, what God will do.

On God's Word we can truly stand.
It says we will go to that Promised Land.
God's Word is forever true.
Find in it what God has for you.

God's Word will never pass away.
It is here to stay.
We can always count on His Word.
Now we must proclaim it until all have heard.

Inspirational Poems of Encouragement

MASTER PLAN

It was planned that Christ would die;
God and the Prophets could not lie.
All the time there was a Master plan.
Who can cause this to work out? God can.

The Master plan finally came to be:
Christ died for you and me.
No other sacrifice would do;
It could not come about by me or you.

No other plan had so thoroughly been thought out,
And Christ only could bring it about.
This plan was harsh, but needful and good.
If anyone could fulfill it, Christ could.

This plan was talked about long ago,
When…I just don't know.
It was a plan concerning you and me.
Christ knew no one else could make it be.

This plan is for all people, all races.
They can't hear if it isn't preached in all places?
This plan we must take to everyone,
And tell them about Jesus, God's Son.

Without God's plan we would be doomed,
And by our own sins we would be consumed.
But in the plan God had considered this:
The blood would cleanse, His way we would not miss.

The plan worked out very well.
Now in Heaven we can dwell.
God has prepared for us a place.
The Master plan: Jesus would save us by His grace.

Inspirational Poems of Encouragement

CAN THIS REALLY BE TRUE

Jesus, are You really real?
Can you make a difference in my life I can feel?
How can even You make such a change?
My life can You rearrange?

I know nothing about how to get in touch with You.
If I say "I'm sorry", will that do?
I want what little about You I have heard.
How will I know if it has occurred?

My life of sin I want to quit,
My life to You, if I can, I want to commit.
I know of no one else to turn to but You.
Lord, can this really be true?

What I have heard is such good news.
I give to you my life, if it you can use.
I am tired of the way I live,
Will You forgive?

My life to You I want to give.
You know my heart, for You I want to live.
Some say from sin You can set free.
If that is the way You do it, will You accept me?

Changing Your life I will gladly do.
For the whole world I would like to do the same thing too.
I died so all can be set free.
I give life to those that come to me.

I have heard what you had to say.
I will accept you just that way.
All that come to me I never turn away.
So come just as you are today.

Inspirational Poems of Encouragement

I CAME

Long ago I came to the earth.
I came to give life, the new birth.
I came for all people of every nation.
So God and man could have a good relation.

I came to save the sinner.
I came to make you a winner.
And to make the weak strong
And to right the wrong.

I came to fix the mess Adam made;
To cleanse from sin, the price I have already paid.
I came to bring righteousness and set man free,
So in sin he would not forever be.

I came to heal the broken hearted,
To bring man back to the way he started.
I came to give man hope,
And grace so he could cope.

A second chance I came to give.
I came and died so he could live.
Giving him good things; it is My pleasure:
Life without end, love and joy without measure.

I came to bless those in need.
I came with God's Word; I sowed good seed.
I came to give not to take.
I came to do good for man's sake.

I came to tell you God loves you.
I came and did what God told Me to do.
One thing more to you I might say,
When you need Me, ask when you pray.

Inspirational Poems of Encouragement

WHAT MORE COULD HE DO

What more could He do than what He has already done?
He could see the race we would run.
There will be obstacles we must face;
Jesus will be by your side as we continue the race.

Is there anything too hard for Him to do?
He will always be there for you.
If worry and doubt cloud your mind,
Bring them to Jesus, He is the greatest find.

Do you ever feel He has forsaken you?
He died for you, what more could He do?
He will be with you to the very end,
Because He is your greatest friend.

To Jesus you can confess your all;
He will surely be there when you call.
Even if the answer isn't today or tomorrow,
He will be there in your time of sorrow.

What more can He do? On Him your troubles cast.
The love He has for you will always last.
He will be there when your best friend leaves;
He loves you, and knows when someone grieves.

What more then could He do
Than always being there for you?
You wonder why these things happen to me,
But with you Christ will always be.

He will go through the valley of death with you,
So what more could He do?
Always remember, Jesus is your best friend.
He says, "I will be with you always, even to the end".

Inspirational Poems of Encouragement

YOU ARE GONE

The struggles in my life sure have been hard,
And the way to You, Lord, seems to be barred.
To find You I have tried and tried.
No longer does it seem we are in stride.

Are you really gone forever?
Would I forsake You? Never.
You said You are the same yesterday and today,
But I can't seem to find You, to my dismay.

I thought it was You I could depend on.
Now it seems You are gone.
As I lay there thinking upon my bed,
No more tears are left I can shed.

Am I in this condition forever to stay,
While You are somewhere else enjoying the day?
Are You so involved there is no time left for me?
I need help, too, but that You must not see.

I wish You would soon return,
So Your Spirit in my heart again would burn.
Have You really forsaken me?
Don't You remember how good our relationship used to be?

I never thought I would face these things without You.
To help me I thought You were supposed to do.
I am afraid when I think I am all alone,
And You not around to help me, but You are gone.

I am not gone as you suppose.
I have never been nearer than I am now.
The greatest victory is just ahead.
You aren't, and never will be, alone.

Inspirational Poems of Encouragement

SO DARK AND BLEAK

My life has had so much pain and toil.
How I wish I had been planted in the soil.
Why couldn't life have been without so much pain?
Lord, will there ever be a touch from You again?

I wish the door would have been left ajar.
But from me You have stayed afar.
Do you enjoy staying so far away?
Won't You answer my question, now-- today?

If I had only died long ago,
Then all this suffering I would not know.
Did I ever quit when there was a battle to fight?
Then why am I left alone to face the night?

I have wondered, Lord where did You go?
I wish I knew the reason; I would like to know.
If only You would come to me and speak.
I could understand why things are so dark and bleak.

Lord, are You ever going to return?
Will "where are You?" in my mind forever burn?
Why did everything turn out this way?
Won't You come and make it a brighter day?

I can't imagine You forever forsaking me.
I know how kind and tender You can be.
Now, I know I was wrong in what I thought.
Because I know what Your Word taught.

You were never alone for an hour.
Each day to overcome I gave you the power.
Others watched to see what you would do.
You won, I was always with you.

Inspirational Poems of Encouragement

SHATTERED HOPES

Do you wonder if you are far from God or near?
If you are by His side or far in the rear?
Are these things ever going to end?
Or, has God become your foe instead of your friend?

Is your life like a tornado that just passed through,
And it is so shattered you don't know what to do?
Is there no way out of this situation I am in?
Is it going to continue the way it has been?

Has there been a spiritual drought that seems like years,
You have prayed, and your eyes stay filled with tears,
Is there no relief from all this pain?
Will I ever get back to a normal life again?

Lord, why can't there be more ups than downs?
Why can't there be more smiles than frowns?
Won't you come today and visit me,
So I won't feel alone, that You I might see?

It seems so long since I heard You speak,
And yet day after day, after You I did seek,
This pain has been there for so long,
I wish just for one day it was gone.

When your life comes together again,
You can help others with a new life to begin,
Don't think those things you went through are for naught,
Through it all to follow Jesus you have sought.

Now Lord, not just me but all those that are hurting today,
Give peace and comfort to them as they go on their way,
And others with their pain, that I might know what to say,
To tell them to trust in Jesus; there is coming a better day.

Inspirational Poems of Encouragement

BY FAITH

By faith the worlds were made,
The trees blossomed and gave us fruit and shade.
By faith the sun was created and it gives us light,
And it separated day from night.

By faith all things in their orbit turn,
So much about God's creation we still learn.
By faith God hung the worlds in space,
By faith each one stays in its place.

The heavens are of old,
How all this began in God's Word we are told.
Each day the sun and moon go down,
Each morning they come back around.

By faith God saw everything that is,
He created man just for His.
By faith He created everything He should,
He looked and saw that it was good.

By faith Adam was created from dust,
If only in God he had kept his trust.
We wouldn't be in the mess we are now in,
Because there would be no sin.

By faith children would be born,
But because of sin they grow old and worn.
By faith God knew Adam would sin;
Now there is death where life once had been.

By faith we believe Jesus died on that tree,
By faith from sin we have been set free.
By faith we believe He rose from the dead,
By faith we will be raised up just like He said.

Inspirational Poems of Encouragement

THE ROCK

A long time has the Rock of Ages been around,
In Him salvation I found.
He has known of me from all past ages,
He is there when my battle rages.

One day I made Him my choice.
I now worship Him, I sing and rejoice.
He is my Rock, my firm foundation,
He changed my life, His recreation.

You are that mighty Cornerstone,
Some of Your past You have made known.
No longer do I face life's troubles alone,
You know and deliver Your own.

The Creator became my Savior;
In You my faith does not waver.
You keep me safe from the evil one;
You are Almighty, yet God's Son.

When I call You are always near,
You are my Rock, what have I to fear.
When I stumble on life's rocky ground,
You guide my steps, You keep me homeward bound.

When the devil comes and says "you are mine",
I tell him I belong to Jesus, I am in the vine.
I don't worry about what my future holds,
God's plan for my life He unfolds.

He is the Rock, in whom I trust,
And will until the day I return to dust.
He is Jesus, the One I long to see,
Soon He is coming after you and me.

Inspirational Poems of Encouragement

WHERE DID YOUR LOVE GO?

When I am in the valley and the waters rise,
Let this not be the day of my demise.
When I should rejoice on the mountain top so high,
Even there my soul seems empty and dry.

Can't You see what's happening to me?
Is this the way You want it to be?
You can see what a turmoil my life is in,
And You know it is not because of sin.

Lord, I know there is no one like You.
Why must all these things I go through?
Can't there be a little joy along the way?
Is it going to be worse tomorrow than today?

Can't You see what is going on down here?
Don't You any longer care?
In my eyes is there left one more tear?
So when, Lord, my cry are You going to hear?

You said for us to draw near to You.
That is what I have been trying to do.
When I seek You, You seem to get farther away.
In Heaven are You going to stay?

Lord, where did Your love go?
I wish You would tell me; I sure would like to know.
I wish You would come and tell me what to do.
Do You not know how much I need You?

In Me you have made your abode,
And down life's path we both have strode.
Don't worry about those things you will face;
I will be there with all My power and grace.

Inspirational Poems of Encouragement

SO MANY TIMES

So many times you have thought, why me?
Things you are going through, why God doesn't see?
For you life has sure been tough,
But God made you of the right stuff.

Others have gone through hard times, too.
He didn't forsake them, He brought them through.
Even when I've thought, Lord, where are You?
In His own way, He did what I needed Him to do.

You say, "God no longer cares",
You cried out and He no longer hears.
It has been so long since an answer to a prayer,
And of your need He is not even aware.

You think no one is going through what you are,
And from you God is staying afar.
He doesn't even seem to listen,
And has forgotten about your mission.

There was so much He called you to do.
Now you think He has forsaken you.
You say, "why did it have to turn out this way?"
Still no answers and it is now another day.

You keep hoping today will be the day
When God comes with something to say.
You never seem to get answers when you pray,
And the waiting continues day after day.

I know the thoughts that have been in your mind.
The answer you need, you will find.
The work I gave you long ago,
I have not forgotten, I remember, I still know.

Inspirational Poems of Encouragement

YOU HEARD

Lord, into Your hands I committed my fate.
You removed all my guilt, sin, and hate.
Only You could make such a change in my life,
You removed the bitterness and strife.

I never knew there could be such joy.
I heard about You since I was a boy.
I have found a wonderful peace.
Sin in my life You caused to cease.

Eternal life You have given me.
My eyes You opened so I could see.
By Your death I have been set free.
No longer darkness in my life will there be.

Without You, life would not be worth living.
I asked and You were so forgiving.
You came and gave me a new heart.
A different lifestyle You gave me for a start.

I cried out and You heard.
Comfort I now get from Your Word.
It says You love me and You care,
And my burdens You will bear.

We don't have to face our troubles alone.
Your love You have abundantly shown.
Your Word to my heart You made real.
My broken life You came to heal.

My trust is no longer in the things I see.
My hope, my faith, my trust is in Thee.
One day I will never again roam.
I will be with You in my new home.

Inspirational Poems of Encouragement

THE STROKE

Is there someone you love that had a stroke?
On our necks satan tries to place his yoke.
Even in your worst of times make God a must.
In Him always keep your trust.

Through all your grief and pain,
In Him our faith we must retain.
All of our tomorrows Jesus knows,
And each day, His love He shows.

When you are so tired and weary,
It has been so long since your heart was merry,
Jesus will give you new strength to face each day.
And grace when things are so dark and gray.

All of our sorrows Christ brought us through.
And I know He will do the same for you.
It did not cross my mind that He did not care.
So I know your burdens He will help you bear.

One day something else satan will try.
But on Christ we will still rely.
One day his reign on earth will end.
And there by my side will be Jesus my friend.

Can you just look to Jesus in good times and bad?
And when things go wrong, at Him you are mad.
He sees your pain and what you are going through.
And in your darkest hour, He will say, "I love you."

Inspirational Poems of Encouragement

I SHALL NOT WANT

The Lord is my shepherd I shall not want,
His power He uses to bless not to flaunt.
In green pastures He causes me to lie,
I just look up and praise the Most High.
By the still waters He leads me,
At times that is the way I need it to be.
He restores my soul,
So I can reach my goal.

In the path of righteousness He leadeth me,
Because in sin, I chose no longer to be.
The valley of the shadow of death I walk through,
I am no longer afraid, my trust is in You.

Evil I will not fear,
Because You are always near.
For Thou art with me,
Alone I will never be.

Thy rod and staff they comfort me,
Because what I go through You always see.
In the presence of my enemies Thou preparest a table,
To win my battle You make me capable.

Thou anointest my head with oil,
And my enemies You foil.
Over runneth my cup,
So there is plenty to fill others up.

Goodness and mercy shall follow me.
That's the way God intended it to be.
All the days of my life,
You keep me from bitterness and strife.

In His house I will dwell,
And drink from His living well.
And be with Him forever,
And from Him, not even death can sever.

Inspirational Poems of Encouragement

THE BEACON

Look at that old lighthouse standing high on the hill;
It has brought so much joy and many a thrill.
So many people have enjoyed visiting this place,
Where the children ran up and down the hill in a race.

No longer does the light in the lighthouse burn bright.
It is now dark where once it had a light.
No longer do visitors come and go,
For so many of the older ones will miss it so.

Many have enjoyed looking out from its top.
From there the children let their pop cans drop.
Many went there with their children and their wives;
It seemed to bring something special to their lives.

There is no need to walk up the hill anymore.
There is no longer a light burning along that shore.
Why was it closed, because of it getting old?
It is like a statue standing there alone in the cold.

But old memories seem to never die.
They just see the old lighthouse toward the sky.
How many lives did it save?
How many has it kept from a watery grave?

From a life of darkness to light Christ will turn,
And that Light will forever burn.
And to everyone salvation He brought,
When the way to life He taught.

But there is still one lighthouse burning bright.
Christ the Lamb, He said, "I am the light".
So come, that light will never steer you wrong;
In your heart there can still be joy, and a new song.

He is still that bright beacon standing on the hill;
For the weary traveler it will burn bright still.
He says, "come to Me, from the rocks and the cold…
You are safe now; My arms around you I fold".

Inspirational Poems of Encouragement

ALMOST TOO LATE

The Lord came and I turned Him down,
When all He wanted was to turn my life around.
But He never gave up on me;
He loved me and just wouldn't let me be.

Why He kept trying, I do not know.
In the depths of my sins He still loved me so.
On the scale of sin, very high I would rate,
But what if I had waited until it was too late?

Lord, why did I put off so long coming to You,
When good was what You had in mind to do?
It would have been an awful fate,
If I had waited until it was too late.

How could You put up with my rejection?
I know it was because of Your love and affection.
How much longer, Lord, would you wait,
Before it would have been too late?

How many more times would You have spoken?
How many times Your heart have I broken?
You saw my terrible state.
Would you try again before it was too late?

I'm glad I finally made Jesus Lord that day.
Now He will be with me each step of the way.
I am so glad You never gave up on me,
And You just wouldn't let me be.

Only You could change my heart,
And take away sin that was keeping us apart.
Thank You, Lord, that I am now forgiven.
To make up time, give me the Spirit to be driven.

Inspirational Poems of Encouragement

I NEED TO KNOW

I need to know if those things I've heard about You are true.
I need to know if those things You did do.
I need to know what this is all about.
Because in my mind, there remains a doubt.

I need to know if in all this You had a hand.
And if You did create the seas and the land.
Or if all this came about by chance.
And over time, things began to advance.

I need to know if You are real.
If You did touch people and heal.
I need to know if sins You can forgive.
And to know if You did raise the dead and they live.

I need to know what good it would do to die on a tree.
Why God would want this to be.
I need to know because something like this I cannot see.
And to know what good all this would do me.

I need to know why You would care.
And how Your life with me You could share.
I need to know why this You would do.
I just need to know if all this is true.

The scriptures about Me the prophets wrote were not lying.
Search them; they tell of My birth and dying.
A sacrifice is required; it you could not give.
So I had to die, or you could not live.

About all this you want to know.
All these things I did long ago.
I did suffer and die on that tree.
All because I love thee.

Inspirational Poems of Encouragement

WOULD MEAN SO MUCH

Just to feel Your presence would mean so much,
Even to the smallest little touch.
At times You seem so far away,
Why do You go off and stay?

There are times of difficulty we go through,
And I wonder sometimes why about that too.
Why does it seem I have been forsaken?
And even my faith is shaken.

What have I done that caused You to leave?
Did I do something that caused You to grieve?
Then why so suddenly were You gone?
Lord, what is wrong?

You said You wouldn't leave; it doesn't seem that way.
I can't seem to get in touch with You when I pray.
When I call why have You not heard?
I cry out, yet You utter not a word.

So Lord, when are You going to return?
Should there be a reason for concern?
To feel Your presence I so desperately need.
My cry, won't You now heed?

How much longer, Lord, will You be gone?
I am so tired and weary, can I go on?
You have been away for so long,
Why won't You return; why are You still gone?

I know you think I went away.
But I was looking after you day after day.
Through it all you stayed on course,
I am and always will be your source.

Inspirational Poems of Encouragement

MY PAST

My trust is in the One who will always be.
He is keeping a close watch over me.
God's grace and love will always last,
So I don't worry about my past.

In God I have kept my faith and trust.
I look to Him for my daily strength; I must.
To God, I have learned to hold fast.
No need to worry about my past.

One day for God I made my stand.
You keep me by Your mighty hand.
God and the world…what a contrast!
I chose God; so I don't worry about my past.

The Lord gave me life; now I can rejoice:
All because I made Him my choice.
One day the earth will burn with fire and a blast.
So I don't worry about my past.

The Lord keeps me: body, mind and soul.
One day I will look around; I have reached my goal,
Because on Him my sins I cast.
Now, I no longer worry about my past.

One day I will no longer tread this earthly path.
I will not be here when God pours out His wrath.
In Christ, I am steadfast;
I no longer worry about my past.

You are my shield, my fortress, my salvation.
The earth one day will lose its gravitation.
Then with You I will be at last.
My failures are now gone, they were part of my past.

Inspirational Poems of Encouragement

I AM

Our God, hope of salvation,
You brought about a great transformation.
My sins kept me bound,
Until deliverance in You I found.

Christ said, "I am the way.
Come and I will give you life today.
I am the truth.
Serve me in the days of thy youth.

I am the resurrection and life.
Come; rid yourself of sin and strife.
I came to bring light,
All over the world it is beginning to shine bright.

Enter in by the door.
You will find salvation and so much more.
I am the true vine.
Come and drink of the new wine.

I am thy high tower.
I give to you grace and power.
I am thy buckler and shield;
Your life, to me yield.

I am the chief cornerstone.
When I came the people should have known.
The stone the builders rejected
Is the one they should have selected.

I am the bright and morning star.
I died, in my side shows the scar.
I am the one the prophets said would come;
Yes, I am the one."

Inspirational Poems of Encouragement

ON JUDGMENT DAY

On Judgment Day and before God you stand.
What will your defense be; what evidence is at hand?
What will God find when He opens the books?
Will He say what you want to hear when He looks?

Will sorrow show on His face?
Has your life been a disgrace?
Is He sad when He sees what is written there?
Was your life empty and bare?

Did you take His birth as just a fable?
He never existed, never born in a stable?
Or, that He was just a mortal,
And never came from Heaven's portal?

During those years of grace, did you repent?
To redeem us; to the earth Christ was sent.
Did you invite Him into your heart?
Christ has been waiting to give you a new start.

What if the last opportunity has now past?
And before God you stand at last.
What will you say to Him on Judgment Day?
You thought your life was okay.

Now, what will you do when before God you stand?
What did you do with Jesus' outstretched hand
On Judgment Day, will you hear, "Well done!"
Or, "Depart from Me, you rejected My Son"?

In eternity, is Heaven the place you will be?
God wants us there, you and me.
What will you do with Jesus while it is yet today?
Remember, there is no other way!

Inspirational Poems of Encouragement

SINS OF AMERICA

The sins of America have become so great:
So much violence, killing and hate.
In everything we are trying to put You out.
Serving You is what America is all about.

Will one day America for her sins have to pay?
I see no repentance, but sin continues day after day.
America must repent before God can forgive.
Will America ever again for You live?

Has America passed the point of no return?
Has America reached the place, God we now spurn?
We must not continue down the path we are on,
Else judgment comes, and the time to repent is gone.

How can lawmakers say "yes" when God has said "no"?
How can America like this continue to go?
"In God we trust" is what our coins say;
We have left that trust; America has lost her way.

Has the thing America stood for become a sham?
We need to teach about Christ the Lamb.
We must return to God and repent,
Or, the freedom we now enjoy from us be rent.

There is only one way this great land can stand:
Put it back where it belongs, in God's hand.
God has blessed America like no other nation.
How could we have let slip away God and our relation?

What will happen to America if we continue in sin?
When we take God out of our affairs, we will not win.
America must repent and keep its resolution.
God is the answer; He is America's solution.

Church and State,
How can the two you separate?
God must be in everything, He must be in all.
The one He is left out of is headed for a fall.

Inspirational Poems of Encouragement

I WISH

Lord, You hear me when I call,
You catch me when I fall.
I wish I had always been perfect before Thee,
But You were always there for me.

I wish I could say I have always pleased You,
But this I could not do.
I wish I could say I have always obeyed,
But the price of obedience I have not always paid.

I wish I could say: You I do not grieve,
Yet when I do You still don't leave.
You loved me when I was slack.
You blessed me so there was no lack.

I wish I could say I always did what was right,
But still You brought me through my night.
You were there in my time of need
You took my hand to safely lead.

I wish I could say I have always trusted You.
When I didn't, You still brought me through.
Not once did You walk away,
You were always there to this very day.

I wish I could say I have done my best,
But when weary, You gave me rest.
There are times when I stumble.
You pick me up without a grumble.

Even when I wasn't all that I should have been,
You blessed me over and over again.
With all my faults, You never gave up on me.
Maybe there is more work to finish for Thee.

Inspirational Poems of Encouragement

GOD, YET MAN

Jesus came and shed His blood,
Did a miracle on blind eyes with a little mud.
He died so from sin I could be free,
That's what He did for me.

It cost Christ so much to come and die.
He is back with the Father, beyond the sky.
It was needful for Him to come,
Or there would be no salvation for anyone.

Who is like Jesus, God, yet man?
Who is able to do what He can?
He spoke the worlds into being by His word
Now we must teach it until all have heard.

One day Christ will rule from sea to sea,
What a wonderful place this earth will be.
God's glory one day will fill the earth;
All will enjoy it that have experienced the new birth.

During the millennium satan will be in the pit for awhile,
He will not roam the earth or walk down the church aisle,
But be bound a thousand years.
We will be with Christ, no more tears.

The time will come when Christ, God's Son,
Will rule the earth; righteousness has won.
We will be with Him. Plenty of time to rejoice,
You will be glad if you made Him your choice.

One day the last war will be fought,
Your suffering will not have been for naught.
With the saints He will forever reign.
There will be a new earth, no more death or pain.

Inspirational Poems of Encouragement

A REASON

There was a reason Christ came to earth that day.
The world was dying; it must not remain that way.
Sin ruled on the earth in which we live,
To free man, His own life He had to give.

Christ spoke God's Word. They would not hear.
He healed the sick, but still did not fear.
He preached the truth. Some did believe,
And those that did, eternal life they did receive.

Who has ever been like this man from Galilee?
He created the earth just for you and me.
For His pleasure the worlds were created.
One day far above them all, we will be elevated.

Who is like this man that all things He knows?
And keeps an eye on the way everything goes.
He knows what a mess this world is in,
All because of sin.

Once America was a bright light for all to see,
But has forgotten God. Why did we let this be?
We must return to the One that can make it right
And once again, for God, it could be a light.

The One who hung the planets in space:
On judgment day before Him we must face.
Look after the earth; we fouled it up for Him.
He must bring light; the earth had grown so dim.

I love this Man that came down from above.
For man He had such compassion and love.
He was the great Creator,
Who then became our Savior.

Inspirational Poems of Encouragement

LOST

I was lost, wandering here and there,
Lost, not even seeming to care.
Lost, until Jesus spoke to me one day;
Hey . . . that's the wrong way.

Lost, didn't know what lay ahead.
Lost, didn't know anything about what God said,
Had Jesus ever spoken to me before now?
When, how?

Lost, on my way to hell,
Lost, not knowing long ago from grace man fell.
Lost, didn't know for my sins Jesus came to pay,
Lost, until Jesus showed me He was the way.

Lost, not knowing which way to go,
Lost, without anyone letting me know.
Lost, not knowing I didn't have to travel life's road along,
The way I had not been shown.

Lost, with no one to share;
Lost, with no one to care.
Lost, not knowing the One that died for me,
Lost, not knowing there was a better way life could be.

Lost, not knowing I was on the wrong track,
Lost, not knowing in my life there was such a lack.
Lost, not knowing God's Word,
Lost, not having ever heard.

But now I finally know,
That Jesus loved me so.
Loved me when I was lost,
Loved me and showed me how much it cost.

Inspirational Poems of Encouragement

DON'T WORRY

In a battle with satan you are now engaged.
He is losing, he is outraged.
He fought hard against you.
He didn't plan on God being there too.

There will be battles you have to fight.
But you will win; you will put satan to flight.
God has planned it; he will lose;
Because righteousness you did choose.

Sometimes you feel you are fighting all alone,
And you are weary to the bone.
Now, satan thinks you he can beat,
But soon finds himself in full retreat.

When satan comes with his weapons of war,
Grace and more grace God will give you more.
Against you he will do all the evil he can,
But God will foil his plan.

There is no battle too big for God and you.
Satan will get so mixed up he won't know what to do.
The battle sometimes seems so hard and long,
But one day the memory of it will be gone.

Never let the battle get you down,
God will help you to stand your ground.
He is always closer than you know;
The battle will turn, your way it will go.

Don't worry when the battle is raging;
I will give you victory, start engaging.
When it seems satan is winning do not fret,
Together we have not lost a battle yet.

Inspirational Poems of Encouragement

KING OF GLORY

Come; see where the King of Glory was born today;
In a stable where animals stay.
He wasn't born in a palace of gold,
But in a little town where the prophets told.

A different baby He must have been.
From His birth was without sin.
The King of Kings wasn't born in a palace of gold,
But in a stable damp and cold.

An ordinary baby, He was not,
He was born for a purpose; He sure gave a lot.
The greatest King ever born wasn't born in a palace of gold,
But in a stable damp and cold.

The shepherds came to see what this was all about,
At His birth the angels rejoiced with a shout.
The baby in her arms she would gently hold,
He was a King, yet born in a stable damp and cold.

Why would God permit His Son to be born in such a place?
For a king this would be a disgrace.
It would be fitting for Him to be born in a palace of gold;
But the King was born in a stable damp and cold.

There was no room for them in the inn.
No invitation to any home, there were no kin.
This baby should have been born in a palace of gold,
He was the Almighty, yet born in a stable damp and cold.

Before He came to earth, He had ivory for His throne,
With streets of pure gold and walls of precious stone.
And owned all the hills, valleys, silver and gold.
Yet was born in a stable damp and cold.

Inspirational Poems of Encouragement

DO IT GOD'S WAY

Surely we are living in the last days,
People not caring, just going their own ways.
Not realizing one day before God they must stand,
Those that rejected His outstretched hand.

We have a form of godliness but deny His power,
What excuse will we use in that hour?
We will give an account of all that we do,
If good or bad, how about you?

Are we so wise, yet not know the truth?
Christ wants us to serve Him from our youth.
Are we so wise we no longer take God by faith?
We no longer need His saving grace?

Can our knowledge free us from sin?
Can our wisdom get us to Heaven, can it get us in?
Man thinks God loves me, He won't send me to hell.
I don't need Him; all will be well.

Have we given thought to what God will say?
Will He say, "Depart from Me" on judgment day?
Why do we not know what is true?
His Word tells us what we must do.

Has our knowledge turned us from truth to fable?
Why can't we grasp the truth; why are we not able?
Why is God's Word in our mind so unclear?
Is it because we do not want to hear?

Our knowledge can be turned to good,
When we believe God's Word like we should.
It is for sure we will face God one day;
It can be a glorious day if we do it God's way.

Inspirational Poems of Encouragement

I BELIEVE

Jesus, I believe You were in the beginning with God,
And You created the Heavens where angels trod.
And all things were created by Thee,
You saw how each thing needed to be.

I believe You hung the planets in space,
And each one stays in its assigned place.
No need each day to tell it where to stay,
From the day it was created, remains to this day.

I believe for Your glory they were created,
And everything good You did, the devil hated.
But You are the one with the final say,
Satan will have his final day.

I believe everything from the beginning You knew.
Things were made with precision; You knew what to do.
I believe You created the earth just for man,
And for him You had a wonderful plan.

I believe You were born, laid in a manger,
And to Your own people You were a stranger.
You preached the gospel to all that would hear,
You healed the sick, raised the dead, delivered from fear.

I believe You came and died.
You shed Your blood; You were crucified.
You knew there was no other way to save me;
This is the way it had to be.

I believe You are coming back for us one day,
To catch those that believe on You away.
There will be no death there;
That only happened before we met You in the air.

Inspirational Poems of Encouragement

SOME OTHER TIME, LORD

Oh how those memories keep coming back like a flood.
How the pastor kept preaching about Jesus and the blood.
Sunday after Sunday he would say you must repent.
And the message, I began to resent.

Everyone wanted me to come and my sins confess.
Each day I wanted to hear the message less.
With my parents to church I would always go.
They hoped one day Jesus, I would come to know.

As time kept going by,
My mother continued to pray for me and cry.
She was worried what my future without God would be.
I wanted to be great, that is what I wanted for me.

There was so much in life I wanted to do.
Some other time, Lord, I will have more time for You.
I have big plans that lie ahead.
One day, I will repent, that is what You said.

I kept postponing those things I knew were right.
And from a child, from Your call I made my flight.
I wanted success that is what I was interested in.
I often thought where I was headed while living in sin.

I made it to the top, the place I wanted to reach.
I remember what my pastor used to preach.
Lord, I have had a wasted life for You.
I knew what was right; what You wanted me to do.

The time would come, I believe,
When Jesus into my heart I would receive.
But I don't seem to feel the tugging I once felt in my heart.
I wish I would have listened, Lord, from the very start

2 Corinthians 6:2

"Now is the accepted time, behold, now is the day of salvation."

Inspirational Poems of Encouragement

WAIT ON YOU

Make me the best soldier I can be,
Fighting battles until there is victory.
And be faithful and true,
Because only my best will do.

Doing my best I won't let You down,
When I was lost You searched until I was found.
I can't be content sitting in my chair,
But be busy for You as long as I am here.

There is so much yet to do.
Helping the poor, sending missionaries for You.
Never losing sight of people who still must hear;
Jesus died; no need to live in fear.

We must work while it is yet day,
Helping those who are struggling along the way.
I know I have not always done my best for You,
But You still forgave, because You wanted to.

There are times I don't know what else to do;
I just pray and wait on You.
And take my stand until the next step I must take.
And study Your Word for my own sake.

Your will for long, You will not conceal,
But in due time will reveal.
I won't worry about what next to do;
There is someone to lend a helping hand to.

Your Word must be heard by every ear;
Not one soul should there be that does not hear.
But perhaps soon You will come,
Then those prepared will go…everyone.

Inspirational Poems of Encouragement

THE GRAVE

Those that die in Christ are not dead but sleeping,
And all the while your soul He is safely keeping.
There is nothing for you to worry about;
The body will come out of the grave with a shout.

The grave couldn't hold Jesus; neither can it hold me.
Jesus gave me a promise that is the way it will be.
Those that die in Christ there is no need for sorrow;
The resurrection might be on the morrow.

It is only the body that is in the grave;
If I die eternal life to me He already gave.
While the body is in the grave sleeping,
I am in Heaven, rejoicing, not weeping.

The grave won't be able to hold me there;
The earth of its dead will be stripped bare.
The grave is only a temporary place;
I prepared not to stay there by God's grace.

At death, remember you are not really dead,
But already enjoying the things that lie ahead.
At death I am just beginning to live,
Because, long ago, His own life He came to give.

The grave is only a resting place for a few days,
I chose God for my life and His ways.
So grave, don't think it will be there for long;
I will be back to pick it up, singing a new song.

One day the grave will have to let me go,
It will have lost its power, God said so.
This earthly life has now past,
Body and Spirit are home with Christ at last.

Inspirational Poems of Encouragement

IT WAS ENOUGH

Through His wounds our Savior bled,
Not another drop of blood need be shed.
Enough was shed to cleanse every heart;
And all who believe on Him, a new life will start.

We no longer need the blood of bulls and goats;
Neither can our sins be hid behind our cloaks.
We need the blood of God's perfect lamb,
Not the sacrifice of a ram.

Christ, the perfect sacrifice was slain,
And in another man's tomb, He was lain.
He wasn't long in the grave;
To sin we no longer are a slave.

He died for all so all could live.
His own life, He came to give.
There was no other sacrifice that would do;
This one was enough for the world, for you.

The blood of an animal could never take away sin;
It had to be offered over and over again.
The prophets spoke of the One that was to come;
It was a sacrifice sufficient for everyone.

This is the only sacrifice God will show respect.
Anything else He would not accept.
Works without Him will not do,
This sacrifice was prepared just for me and you.

We must believe it was enough once and for all,
Now He wants to place in every heart, His call.
Yes, Jesus came and died,
He now sits on God's right hand…Glorified.

Inspirational Poems of Encouragement

WHEN FIRST WE DID MEET

How long have I waited for an answer to a prayer?
When I pray, are You even aware?
Forever, is that how long I must wait?
At the bottom, with You, I must rate.

I once had some self esteem;
I was in love with God…Supreme.
Why are things so bad; when it was so sweet?
Like it was when first we did meet?

Nothing seems to go right,
When I cry out, You shut the door tight.
When I call upon Your Name
"No" must be my answer, nothing is the same.

Is the door to Heaven ever going to open again?
How do I get in touch with You; how do I begin?
When I call You never seem to hear;
Away from me, You turn Your ear.

Anymore You must never be around.
When I search, You can't be found.
I sure struggle, having to make it on my own;
Far away, You must have flown.

I come as I always have, hoping to be heard;
When I prayed, I used to feel assured.
But now I hear nothing when I pray.
You seem to have vanished, nothing You have to say.

You never have to live your life in fear.
My Spirit is in your heart, be of good cheer.
Problems in life may seem to never end,
But I will always be your very best friend.

TRUE TO MINE

God's Word shows us of His ways.
His love for us lasts all of our days.
He never grows tired of our seeking Him.
He never forgets to bless us.

Our time with Him is a pleasure,
Because we love and adore Him.
He never gets tired of our praise,
Each day He looks forward to our worship.

Do we give Him all the praise He is due?
He came and died that you could live.
More blessings to you He wants to give,
He is God, and has plenty to offer.

Do you have what He wants to give you?
He has what you are seeking, if you ask.
His supply never gets low,
It just grows and grows.

He says, "Ask and you will receive",
That is just one of His delights.
But our praise we must not forget.
That, too, is part of our worship.

Never grow weary when things go wrong,
He will work it out; you will be strong.
He will "never forsake you", is His Word,
I have always found it to be true.

In Him I have put my trust;
He has never let me down.
He has stood true to His Word;
Now I must be true to mine.

Inspirational Poems of Encouragement

IF THERE WAS NO FORGIVENESS

If there was no forgiveness,
Then there would be no hope.
In life I could not cope,
If Christ had said nope.

If there was no forgiveness,
In darkness I would always be.
The light of Christ I would never see,
Sin would always have its hold on me.

If there was no forgiveness,
In sin I would always be.
Eternal life I would not see,
At death Christ would not welcome me.

If there was no forgiveness,
A part of God's family I could never be.
From sin I could not be free;
Sin would be in control of me.

If there was no forgiveness,
Then Christ I would never see.
No joy would there be in me,
In Heaven I would never be.

If there was no forgiveness
His fellowship I would never know.
In Christ's likeness I could not grow,
And to Hell I would surely go.

Christ did not leave us without forgiveness;
He came and set me free from sin.
It will not be part of my life ever again;
I have been forgiven; now Christ dwells within.

Inspirational Poems of Encouragement

ALL THIS HELL

Why does life have to be so much hell?
Is there a reason, won't You come and to me tell?
This sure must be what they call hell on earth.
It has come against me for all it is worth.

Have you been through my hell?
Then how can you say all will be well?
If you do not understand,
How can you say on your feet you will land?

These years of hell, is there nothing You will do?
It seems not even You I can turn to.
Won't You come and show me You care?
When I call why do You not hear?

Why Lord don't You answer my prayer?
This burden, won't You come and help me bear?
Why are You waiting so long to help me?
All this hell can't You see?

These many years; how many more must there be,
Before You come down to take a look and see?
Isn't it time there was a break from this for me?
Why are You continuing to let this be?

Over the years in my hell I know I did complain.
My friends tried hard to explain.
I know they prayed and did their best.
Maybe they are praying when they need to rest.

Things are now getting better I can see.
The light at the end of the tunnel is waiting for me.
It is losing its hold that has been my hell.
And I do believe, soon I also can say all is well.

Inspirational Poems of Encouragement

ECHOES OF TIME

Were poems planned for me way back in the echoes of time?
Maybe You also had lines written that would rhyme.
Would You show me if You did?
Or would it be something from me forever hid?

To all my questions, an answer you could easily give,
Because from everlasting to everlasting You did live.
What were You thinking all the way back in time?
Were You thinking of my sublime?

I wish I knew what You were doing way back then,
And know a little about when all this began.
When I get to Heaven this I might never know,
But I am sure there will be a lot of things to us You will show.

Was Lucifer Your first creation back then?
His voice sounded all through Heaven when his singing began.
Back then was the earth already hung in space,
Or was it only a thought, not yet a trace?

Since you have been around from so long ago,
You have kept everything in order and under control.
Lord, all these questions I leave up to You,
But I still wonder about these things too.

Back then were there beings of any kind?
At this time was I already on Your mind?
Was there anyone You loved then as much as You do man?
Was there anyone to love You as man can?

If I was with You, would these things I even want to know,
Or just wherever You went I would want to go?
But if I never know what took place way back then,
All that matters I will be with You until I don't know when.

Inspirational Poems of Encouragement

WHEN HE COMES I WILL GO

Jesus came and preached, "You must be born again".
Then a new life in Him will begin.
I repented of my sins now I know
That when He comes, I will go.

Jesus went through much for us to go to that Promised Land.
Outstretched to you is that nail-scarred hand.
Will you take it or let it go?
He loves you and wants you to know.

But the choice He leaves up to you.
The right thing He hopes you will do.
The choice for eternal life He wants you to make.
His preaching was plain, so there would be no mistake.

He didn't have to come and die.
But our sins compelled Him that is why.
Such love for the sinner was never known.
So Jesus died, now it was shown.

The price for your pardon Christ paid.
A place in Heaven for us He has made.
His love do you know?
When He comes, will you go?

We now have His Word that He taught.
He paid the debt for our sins, it could not be bought.
I chose not to go to that place below.
My life to Him I gave, now when He comes I will go.

Come to Jesus, He has a much better life for you.
Saving sinners is what He loves to do.
One day He is coming after those born again.
Will you go and life with Him begin?

Inspirational Poems of Encouragement

PATIENCE WEARING THIN

The toils of life have worn my patience thin.
It sure is terrible the way things have been.
I didn't know it would be like this,
But most of all, Your presence is what I miss.

Lord, there is so much to face along the way.
Won't You come with just a word for me today?
I just wish I could see a speck of light,
So I would know it is the end of my night.

Is it possible all this will change for me today?
I have prayed and don't know what else to say.
I will obey, if only You will show me what to do.
How much longer before I hear from You?

I want my trust to remain in You,
But I just don't know what else I can do.
I don't mind going the extra mile,
If on Your face there would be a smile.

Is this going to continue on this way,
Or is it going to be worse than today?
Then I just pray for Your grace.
Not to grow weary with the things I face.

When will I be free from all this pain?
When will You come and visit me again?
I know in Your timing You will see me through,
But oh how hard it is while waiting on You.

When you are awake or while you are asleep,
My grace is sufficient; you it will safely keep.
In Me you have kept your trust and obeyed,
And through it all, you were never swayed.

Inspirational Poems of Encouragement

PICKING ON ME

Why, Lord, is it me You are always picking on?
I don't think I am always doing wrong.
Why can't I once in awhile get a break?
Why must something go wrong when I awake?

You know my hurts; but You leave me this way?
They never cease, night or day.
You know I have always loved You.
Why not come and something about this do?

Why, Lord, from me do You want to flee?
You know I am weak and frail compared to Thee.
This has been going on for so long, You can see.
So why is it taking so long to come and help me?

My troubles won't You come and take?
I need help; won't You come just for my sake?
If not, then just let me be.
You no longer seem to care about me.

Won't You ease this pain if only for one night?
From my pain, why do You take Your flight?
Through Your stripes we are healed, just let that be,
And not forsake me.

Lord, these things keep persisting day after day.
Far away You seem to stay.
Won't You just let up for a little bit?
Won't You give me peace I need it?

Have I been wrong? It didn't seem that way to me.
But if this was for another reason that I did not see,
Forgive me for looking at it this way.
I repent Lord, and ask for forgiveness today.

Inspirational Poems of Encouragement

TANGLED IN SATAN'S WEB

I know You came to this earth to die,
But I sometimes wonder why.
You could have created another race,
Then death You would not have to face.

The earth now had sin, create another place,
And a people that would obey, not spit in Your face.
You chose this one, now You would have to die.
To save a people that about You would lie.

You told Adam what not to do,
But he did not obey You.
Sin changed the whole situation;
But You still loved Your creation.

You saw the state man was in,
All because of Adam's sin.
It shouldn't have turned out this way.
The penalty for sin, You had to pay.

Man was at his lowest ebb,
Bound by sin, tangled in satan's web.
You came to die and forgive,
So those under the penalty of death could live.

Man, himself he could not save.
It took the spotless Son of God, His life He gave.
This is the only sacrifice you will ever need.
You can have life if God's Word you heed.

Jesus wants to turn your life around,
To sin you no longer have to be bound.
From the lowest of low He will lift you up;
Because He already drank from that awful cup.

Inspirational Poems of Encouragement

WITH YOU THE ANSWER STAYED

How many times have I sought You and prayed?
Waited, but with You the answer stayed.
I know God says He hears,
Yet, day after day, I live with my fears.

I pray, yet, at times I don't know,
Did my prayer get through, did it go?
Because when I prayed,
With You the answer stayed.

For the answer I continue to wait,
Will the answer come? Will it be late?
I have believed, prayed,
Yet, with You the answer stayed.

I pray, so why am I not sure?
Will I make it, can I endure?
Because when I prayed,
With You the answer stayed.

It has been so long since I heard;
I searched for an answer in Your Word.
Lord, why wasn't there an answer when I prayed?
I ask, but with You the answer stayed.

From me is Your Spirit gone?
Lord, has He been withdrawn?
I longed for an answer when I prayed,
Still with You the answer stayed.

I was there when there was no song,
I was there with you all along.
I was there when you prayed,
And when you thought with Me the answer stayed.

Inspirational Poems of Encouragement

YOU WILL WIN

Lord, When will things get better for me again?
Won't a new refreshing day ever begin?
How much more before you know I love You?
This situation won't I ever get through?

On earth I went through much for you.
So I do understand what you are going through.
Be not troubled or dismayed.
The price for everything you need I have paid.

Sometimes you will wonder why this has to be.
Just rejoice; lift up your voice in praise to Me.
One day there will be no more pain or worry.
I know you wish it would hurry.

Satan will convince many this is of Me,
He will say, yes, this was He.
Why, these things to you would I do?
When I suffered, so from them I could deliver you.

Satan would like for you to disappear from earth,
He wishes you had never known of the new birth.
He would like to destroy you,
But this he cannot do.

Satan, you never have to fear;
When you call I am always near.
I will never leave you I have said.
I am not in the grave; I am not dead.

When satan comes with all his power,
Do not be disheartened in that hour,
You will win; the battle is Mine.
Through it all, let your light shine.

Inspirational Poems of Encouragement

YOU ASK NO LESS

The Lord has always been good to me,
He has blessed in ways I did not see.
And mercies that were never shown,
And love I had not known.

His love is too great to fully comprehend,
His blessings He doesn't withhold; He is our friend.
He gives to us without measure,
And His goodness He gives for our pleasure.

We don't know how God works out His plan,
But He works them out for the good of man.
From long ago I have known of His love.
It is from His heart, gentler than a dove.

He always knows just what we need;
When we pass our blessings on, can be our good deed.
God never forgets the little things we do;
He blesses and gives good things back to you.

Thank You for Your love for me.
We show by our deeds it is of Thee.
It never grows old or stale,
And with His love we cannot fail.

Never let me grow weary of what You want me to do,
But each day seek something new.
You always have new ways to refresh,
And blessings untold to bless.

So each day I just worship You with praise.
I want to be on fire for You, set me ablaze,
To do my best, You ask no less,
But when I fail, You still love me and bless.

Inspirational Poems of Encouragement

A LITTLE TASTE OF HEAVEN

God gives us a taste of Heaven here.
When we feel His presence and know He is near.
One day in Heaven in all its glory we will be.
But now, a little taste of Heaven He gives me.

He came, told about hell so we would not go,
And talked about Heaven so we would know;
But with a taste of Heaven, we are now blessed.
One day we will be Heaven's eternal guest.

We know little about Heaven, but we might soon see
How wonderful God has prepared it for you and me.
But we can have a little taste of Heaven now,
If our sins we confess, and before Him bow.

Who knows when He will come to take us there?
No more burdens, sorrows, death, or care.
But a taste of Heaven He now gives.
One day we will be there, where God lives.

Oh, what a difference from the old body to the new.
But that won't keep me from knowing you.
For now only a little of Heaven, He lets me taste.
I must let Him use my life, that it be not a waste.

One day in Heaven, what we longed for will become real.
But here, He gave us life for death -- what a deal!
For now only a taste of Heaven will there be.
But more than a little taste of Heaven is awaiting me.

One day to Heaven with Him we will go.
Then, what Heaven is like we will know.
But for now only a little taste of Heaven do we get.
For our goal we still haven't reached yet.

Inspirational Poems of Encouragement

CAUGHT UP

Soon I will be caught up to meet the Lord in the air.
No more sickness, suffering, or despair.
Maybe even death I will not see,
Because to my new home He is taking me.

Then, things will never be the way they were,
You will not find me here, anywhere.
Because I will be caught up, I will be over there;
Nothing here can compare.

We will be gone in the twinkling of an eye;
There will no longer be a need for a goodbye.
Get ready for your reward now;
It will be so wonderful you might say "wow".

When He comes no time to repent,
After those that are ready He is sent.
I am looking for Him to come most any day,
Gravity can't hold me, I will be caught away.

He will be coming for those that are looking;
Christ has already taken care of my booking.
Have you made preparations; is your name in God's book?
One day He will take a look.

Heaven is a place all should want to go.
But a personal relationship with Jesus you must know.
A wonderful place that must be,
And He has a place prepared there for you and me.

He will be coming back one day.
Will you be caught up or here will you stay?
I will not worry about those things I left behind,
Because great things for me God has in mind.

Inspirational Poems of Encouragement

WEARINESS

"Be not weary in well doing" we are told,
Weariness in body also wants to have a hold.
Weariness just seems to creep in;
It all started with Adam's sin.

As I get older, weariness seems to know,
But when time to leave, it is slow.
Weariness sometimes just takes its toll,
But it can't keep me from reaching my goal.

Weariness is a pest and wants to come back,
But God gives me strength, there is no lack.
One day weariness will have to go;
It will be banned from my life; that I know.

Weariness can sure wear you out;
Satan enjoys that, that's what he's all about.
I can still come to God in those times, too.
He refreshes me; He knows just what to do.

Weariness has visited many in its day,
And many more it will visit before it goes away.
One day God will say "go".
That will be a wonderful day, I know.

One day weariness will no longer be,
Jesus will have removed it from you and me.
That word will no longer be;
From getting old, tired, weary I will be free.

When weary in body, God helps us down life's road.
He will be there to help us with our heavy load.
We know one day this will all end,
Because a new life we will begin.

Inspirational Poems of Encouragement

NOW IT IS TOO LATE

They waited for Jesus to come and heal.
Why does he not come at our appeal?
He could have healed before He died.
But now the wrappings have been applied.

Jesus said, "Lazarus is asleep.
Let us go, an appointment with him I must keep."
Then to His disciples He said,
"Lazarus died, I go to raise him from the dead."

Martha said, "Lazarus was sick; he was Your friend.
Now he is dead; why did his life have to end?
Why, so long did you wait?
Now it is too late.

"If you came sooner my brother would not be dead."
"I am the resurrection," Jesus said.
"I know he will be raised at the last day."
"He will rise today, in the grave he will not stay."

There were happy times when Jesus passed through,
But today sorrow has come to this house, too.
Usually there was joy and a good meal to eat,
"Today a mission I must complete."

Jesus came to raise a friend that day;
He brought joy to their house; that was His way.
Maybe they learned something by their wait:
That Jesus was right on time -- He was not late.

When Jesus comes He brings joy.
When Jesus comes He gives peace.
When Jesus comes He brings healing.
When Jesus comes He gives life.

Inspirational Poems of Encouragement

EVERYTHING IS GOING WRONG

Have you ever thought, God where are You?
Won't the time ever come for my breakthrough?
It seems it has been forever.
Even the answer seems to be never.

Many are waiting for an answer to their prayer,
And of Your presence they are unaware.
Why, Lord, do You wait so long
When everything is going wrong?

I sought You, yet I have not heard from You.
Why do You delay? I did all I know to do.
I cry out, "things are so bad,
How long since peaceful days I have had?"

Come, Lord, and peace give to me.
Speak and I will change whatever needs to be.
Just show me what I must do.
Gladly I will obey You.

Why do my thoughts run wild when You're not near?
Why do I wonder what is wrong when You're not here?
If anything in my life that grieves You, remove,
So the things I do and say will improve.

Lord, there are things I need to know;
No one has the answer to whom I can go.
Only in You can I rely;
So, I will wait for Your reply.

Lord, forgive me when I complain.
And from words of doubt refrain.
To serve You with all my heart is my quest;
Then I know You will take care of the rest.

Inspirational Poems of Encouragement

HE IS FAITHFUL AND JUST

Is it possible Jesus could come today?
He just may.
Could you welcome Him back and say,
"Yes, Lord, I am ready, come today!"

I made my decision for Christ in my late teens.
Now make Him your decision, by all means.
Into His hands put now your trust.
You won't be disappointed, He is faithful and just.

Christ wants you to be part of His family, too;
But the decision He leaves up to you.
In Heaven He wants to prepare for you a place,
And give you eternal life by His love and grace.

Life's pathway He doesn't want you to walk alone.
His love for you He has already shown.
Eternal things He wants to give to you,
But you must want them, too.

Don't think you are so bad He won't forgive.
When you repent, a new life you begin to live.
He wants to give you life and more;
A mansion will be waiting on that Heavenly shore.

In Him is not a life of fear.
He is a friend who is always near.
You can talk to him as a dear friend,
And have a relationship that will never end.

He is waiting for you to come to Him now;
One day before Him all must bow.
Soon He will be coming back for His own,
So come, go with me to our Heavenly home.

Inspirational Poems of Encouragement

WHEN WILL YOU VISIT ME?

When will You come and visit me?
The one beside me is getting blessed, You can see.
When will the time of my blessing come?
When will I get a visit from the Holy One?

I have waited so long for my visit to be.
When, Lord, will you come and visit me?
My heart's desire is to serve and worship Thee,
So come now and visit me.

I know You loved me before the world was,
You died; my sins were the cause.
All this shows love is of Thee,
So come and visit me.

My cares You don't come and share,
My burdens You leave for me to bear.
My problems, Lord, don't You see?
So when will You come and visit me?

Why my troubles alone must I face?
While from me You hold Your grace.
There is no one else to come to but Thee.
So come and visit me.

You loved me more than I will ever know,
Because to the cross for sin You had to go.
But right now I sure need Thee,
So won't You come now and visit me?

Lord, You have always been good to me;
Looking back on life I can see.
You said with me You would always be,
So why would I think You have forgotten me.

Inspirational Poems of Encouragement

COMPLAIN

We complain when we should rejoice;
We complain when having to make a choice.
Even toward You, Lord, we complain,
Because You do not remove our pain.

We complain when it is hot and when it is cold.
We complain when there is not enough silver and gold.
We complain when things are good and bad.
We complain about the rotten day we just had.

We complain when things don't go right;
We complain when we have to go on a diet.
We complain when there is no answer when we pray,
Because our troubles do not go away.

We complain when our job doesn't meet our need;
We complain when we ask and God doesn't heed.
We complain when there is really no reason;
We complain the year round; it has no season.

We complain when someone neglects to speak;
We get hurt instead of staying humble and meek.
We complain when we have to wait;
We complain when we run late.

We complain when we should be quiet.
When we complain, in us does God delight?
It must be in our nature to complain,
Because we do it over and over again.

Can we just remember next time not to complain?
Or, are we always in that state going to remain?
When we start to complain, refrain,
God, I know, will help us to restrain.

Inspirational Poems of Encouragement

THOUGHTS

There are thoughts that are good,
Thoughts that are not.
Thoughts on how others we might blame.
Thoughts that glorify Thy Name.

Thoughts that reach the highest Heaven.
Thoughts that are of the lowest hell.
Thoughts that should never be,
Thoughts to worship Thee.

Thoughts that others never know.
Thoughts that only friends you let know.
Thoughts that would be embarrassing if anyone knew.
Thoughts of praise, Lord, to You.

Thoughts you wouldn't want the Lord to know.
Thoughts that are bad for you.
Thoughts that will lift you up,
And thoughts that are corrupt.

Thoughts that you want to express,
Thoughts that you want to depress.
Thoughts you wish you had never thought,
Thoughts of the One who salvation brought.

Thoughts that do you harm,
Thoughts that should cause you alarm.
Thoughts to bless,
And thoughts we need to confess.

Thoughts about my Lord and me,
Thoughts about how salvation came to be.
Thoughts of seeing the One who died for me,
Thoughts of being with Christ for all eternity.

Inspirational Poems of Encouragement

NINE-ONE-ONE

Lord, I pray for America in its time of grief and pain.
Will the hurt ever go away and things be normal again?
Reach down with your healing touch;
And peace give to those that have been through so much.

I pray for our leaders, for the decisions they need to make;
To look to You in what steps they need to take.
To make the right decisions in time of peace and war;
On what to do about what took place on our shore.

Lord, You know what happened on nine-one-one.
You saw the terrible act that was done.
Give our leaders wisdom to know what to do.
For wisdom, it is You we must turn to.

We pray for those who lost husbands, children, wives.
For no reason so many lost their lives.
Bless those that came to help from all over the U.S.A.
For them I also pray.

Serving You is what America is all about.
In all our decisions You must not be left out.
America, Lord, was founded on You.
We must trust in You, in everything we do.

Father, bless America as we fight terror.
And forgive us; we are not always above error.
Nine-one-one is a day we will long remember.
It happened the eleventh day of September.

Lord, it was You that made America great.
Could that be the reason, against us, is so much hate?
One nation, under God, is why America stands.
If it wasn't for You, we would just be like other lands.

Inspirational Poems of Encouragement

THE RIGHT ONE

Why does life have to be like this?
With no family, no children to hug and kiss?
Why don't You smile on me so this will be?
I want the right one, meant just for me.

Why must I face life without the one that is right?
I sure wish I could meet them tonight.
Is this ever going to happen; will this ever be?
There must be a right one, meant just for me.

I have prayed for the right one to come my way.
Yet I keep waiting, day after day.
I have waited this, You must see.
Lord, where is the right one, meant just for me?

Why don't You hear when I pray,
And send that special someone by today?
When will that day, for me, be?
When I meet the right one, meant just for me.

When I call, why is there a delay?
Why is the answer always some other day?
When will the answer to my prayer be?
When You send the right one, meant just for me?

Lord, if there is a reason for the delay,
Then I will accept that as my answer for today.
Your will is the way I want it to be.
So I will wait for the right one, meant just for me.

I believe the Lord has the right one for you.
And perhaps you have done all you know to do.
Trust God, in waiting, in prayer, and tears,
I know He has blessed us with more than fifty years.

Inspirational Poems of Encouragement

WHY OTHERS, NEVER ME?

Life has been like a stormy sea,
Tossing me about, trying to devour me.
The good things in life keep passing me by.
Does it always have to be like this…why?

Why do these things happen to me…why?
Why can't once in a while I see a bright blue sky?
Why does it have to be lightning and thunder?
Why is my life always being torn asunder?

Why can't something good come my way…why?
I try hard; I really try.
Why don't things ever work out for me?
Is this the way it was meant to be?

Why can't a good life for me begin?
These things happen over and over again?
Will things for me ever change?
Will the better things always be just out of range?

Why can't something in my life turn out good?
It seems I have done everything I could.
Why can't my life be like others I see?
Things turn out good for others, why not me?

I want things for me to be better, too.
Why do I fail in whatever I try to do?
Is there no one to help me?
Is this the way it will always be?

There is someone you should know.
He will change your life and show you the way to go.
Jesus is His name. He came to earth to die for man.
He loves you; He will do what no one else can.

Inspirational Poems of Encouragement

THINGS

In You, Lord, I now delight.
I have found the way that is right.
Because You forgave me of a life of sin,
Now You give me grace to overcome and win.

Now I do those things You ask of me.
You taught me what You want me to be.
I seek those things that are of Thee.
To love others, that's what You require of me.

I have always trusted in my own way;
I did until today.
I thought things, if I had, I had succeeded.
But what was most important, I had not heeded.

Why were things so important to me?
Why couldn't I open my eyes and see?
Great, I thought things would make me.
Until the day I met Thee.

Life didn't turn out the way I thought.
Things, not Christ, I sought.
Things did not lead me into righteousness and grace.
Or prepare me to meet the Just One I must face.

After all this time in sin, I now see,
It was You I always needed, not me.
I can't make the changes I need, so I turn to Thee.
I now know where my trust should be.

What advice to you would I give?
Give your life to Christ and live.
He will give what you never had.
It is always good, never bad.

Inspirational Poems of Encouragement

I DIDN'T KNOW

My life for Christ has been a total waste.
Now, what I do for Christ must be with haste.
I didn't know there was any other, way.
I didn't know I could come to You and pray.

No matter where I go or what I do,
Something seems to always go wrong there to.
No matter how hard I try,
If only far away from it all I could fly.

I have wondered *is this what life is all about?*
What in my life have I left out?
If only my troubles I could leave far behind,
And peace, I could find.

Peace, oh, if only that could be.
But, it seems to always elude me.
It would be so good just to know,
If there would be peace some place I go.

There must be a better way of life than this.
There has been little joy, this I miss.
If there could only be one day of peace,
And my problems for that day would cease.

If there could have been peace within,
What a joy that would have been.
If only my troubles would go away,
And peace would come today.

Finally, a change in my life came to be.
Peace came; there was joy, what a difference in me.
The wrong things in my life, God caused to cease.
I now have Christ, and my day of peace.

Inspirational Poems of Encouragement

IF

If You had not died, I could not live.
If I did not repent, You could not forgive.
If You had not come, I could not go.
If You had not shown me the way, I would not know.

If no stripes on your back, I could not be healed.
If You had not brought God's Word, Heaven would not be revealed.
If You had not come, there would be no new birth.
If You had not returned, we could not be the salt of the earth.

If Jesus did not care, hell would be my home.
If Jesus did not love me, a mansion I would not own.
If Jesus had not died, I would always be a sinner.
If Jesus did not rise, I would not be a winner.

If He had not told me, truth I would not know.
If no forgiveness, mercy He could not show.
If He had not come, and preached God's Word;
I would be lost, now there's no excuse, I have heard.

If there was no word, Jesus I would never know.
If He had not come, faith in my heart could not grow.
If there was no cross, I would still be in sin.
If he had not suffered, there would be no peace within.

You did come, now I rejoice in Your love.
You did come; I will be with You in Heaven above.
You did die, now I live.
You're alive, and You forgive.

All my sins You saw, You wiped clean my slate.
You gave me a new life, You changed my fate.
First You had to die; then be raised from the dead.
This all happened, just as Your Word said.

Inspirational Poems of Encouragement

APPEAR IN GOD'S COURT

One day, satan, to hell you will go.
That's what God's Word says, that's how I know.
You had your chance to worship God in praise.
But your voice against Him you begin to raise.

You wanted all the glory and praise.
Why you weren't faithful to God, I am amazed.
You worked hard to turn people from God's way.
That was your joy; that was your heyday.

One day you will pay for what you did.
The earth of you, God will rid.
You could have done what was right,
But you chose to do evil with all your might.

God also gave man the choice of right and wrong.
He had power to overcome, he failed; it was gone.
Satan, you will get what you deserve.
God has a place prepared, held in reserve.

After all this time, you still destroy and kill,
To separate man from God and His will.
You have worked hard at what you are doing;
To keep man in bondage, you keep pursuing.

You had better make use of the time you have left.
God is tired of your theft.
Remember, your time is set and it is short,
And you will appear before God in His court.

One day, God will say, "Enough is enough!"
When God speaks, He does not bluff.
The time will come when it is your last day.
Because of what you did, you will have to pay.

Inspirational Poems of Encouragement

HIS NAME

Jesus is His name, this I know.
Because He lives, I live also.
He died so from sin I could be free.
That's how much He loved me.

One day in Heaven, the Father we will meet,
The church, He will be waiting to greet.
And in all His glory we shall see,
Because with Him we will forever be.

The one the Prophets wrote about…came.
He was not born in wealth or fame.
Around the world His name we now proclaim.
He brought me life, I brought Him shame.

There is so much to say about this Man.
He forgives, gives life; He does what no one else can.
He walked the shores of Galilee,
And taught the people from sin you can be free.

He never changes, but always is the same.
We live to bring glory and honor to His name.
Never has there been a name like His.
No name is worthy of praise, but His is.

One day His name will be known by all.
He died to redeem Man from the fall.
There is no forgiveness but by His name.
When He forgives, your life will not be the same.

If you want eternal life, call upon His name.
We are the cause of His death; sin is to blame.
When he cleanses, you will be whiter than snow.
One day to the City of God we will go.

Inspirational Poems of Encouragement

YOUR DAY BEFORE GOD

Once my prayer life and in God's Word I became slack.
You didn't forsake me, but soon there was a lack.
What I deserved was for You to leave,
But You didn't even though it caused You to grieve.

You knew one day, after You again I would seek.
Because You cared, my soul You did safely keep.
When I drifted off and we were apart,
I was never out of Your thoughts and heart.

If during your life you go astray,
Come back to Christ; there is no other way.
God is waiting for you to repent, so He can forgive.
And give you life once again, so you will live.

Don't think there is more pleasure in sin,
Emptiness one day will come; no peace within.
Don't wait until for sin you have to pay,
You will give account on judgment day.

Now He is waiting for you to return,
And after His will, once again yearn.
But if you wait until it is too late,
Eternity will be an awful fate.

He is waiting for you to say yes.
Don't think; *I have plenty of time*, don't guess.
One day you will stand before God, you have a date.
So come; don't wait.

Christ doesn't want you to be lost.
For your freedom from sin was at a great cost.
Come back now; let Him make you whiter than snow.
So when He comes after the church, you will go.

Inspirational Poems of Encouragement

SEEK ME

Seek Me is what I desire of thee.
Seek Me is the way I want it to be.
Seek Me and know what I want you to do.
And I will reveal things to you.

Seek Me; how close do you want to get?
Seek Me; do you have what you want yet?
Is the inner man still hungry from want?
Don't let your life be lived for naught.

Seek Me and see what I will do.
Seek Me and see what's in store for you.
Seek Me and see if I don't reply,
And pour out blessings on you from My supply.

Seek Me; are you hungry for more?
Seek Me; see what's waiting beyond Heaven's door.
Seek Me; there is still plenty to do.
Let My Spirit work through you.

Seek Me; I will show you things you never knew.
Seek Me and see what I will do with you.
Seek Me; put your faith and trust in Me,
And see if Heaven doesn't open to thee.

Seek Me in good times and bad.
Things you might not understand; one day you will be glad.
Draw near to Me and see what I will do,
And see if blessings don't come to you.

Seek Me; serve and follow Me.
Then one day, with Me you will be.
You won't be sorry for your sacrifices on that day.
Finish your mansion; it is well on the way

Inspirational Poems of Encouragement

I AM SAFE

Thank You for coming into my life and spirit.
Nothing I did or do did life I merit.
Because of Your love and grace,
Eternal death, I no longer have to face

Through every battle You guide my life each day.
My sins You gave Your life to pay.
Now we live in Godly awe,
And in Your Spirit and by Your law.

I just want to come before You with thanks and praise.
And in songs of worship, my voice I raise.
All because of Your love for me,
You hung and died on that ole tree.

No longer do You have to die for sin.
Once You did for all, now a new life can begin.
Maybe at times there seems no joy and peace.
But power to overcome will never cease.

In this world of darkness our light must shine.
We no longer are of the world; we serve the Great Divine.
You have shown Your love and mercy; it was Your will.
When we were unworthy, You loved us still.

Before You came, salvation no one knew.
But the prophets of old prophesied what You would do.
The time came and You must die,
To save someone like me; I have wondered why.

Let me say "thank You" over and over again,
For forgiving me of my sins, and eternal life will begin.
I am now waiting to go to that Promised Land.
In the meantime, I am safe in my Master's hand.

Inspirational Poems of Encouragement

LOST HER WAY

Lord, America has left You out of her affairs.
Are we so far gone; too late for repairs?
In You we no longer have our trust
And have not sought You the way we must.

Father, to You America must return,
And the fire of God in our hearts again burn.
And in Your favor, once again be,
And the way we are headed we could see.

America, Lord, has gone astray.
We have forsaken You and gone our own way.
Come, Lord, and in our hearts once again live.
And our sins forgive.

The God America once knew we have forsaken.
By Your Word we no longer are shaken.
The God we once respected and trusted in
Has been replaced by sin.

America knew her calling; she knew what to do.
Now, we have no time left for You.
It is God America needs; not the pleasures of sin.
Sin makes losers – we cannot win.

America, Lord, has lost her way.
Bring her back on the right path, I pray.
The world once looked at her as a Godly nation,
And with You had a good relation.

America has left its Godly roots.
I pray once again, it would bring forth fruits,
And return to the one that made America strong,
And not wait too long to repent of our wrong.

Inspirational Poems of Encouragement

WHY DID I LET THIS BE?

Long ago when I was a lad,
Living without Christ, lonely, and sad
He knew of me. I knew Him not.
He loved me; it was me that forgot.

Why did I live this way? Why did He still love me?
My life is not the way He wanted it to be.
He had a much better life than this for me.
Then why did I wait so long and let this be?

Sin in my life is what I chose.
But something better, God did propose.
He left nothing good out of His plan for me.
Why did I wait so long and let this be?

Maybe He wondered why His offer I did not take.
I realize now what a grave mistake.
But His love did not waiver for me.
Why, so long, did I let this be?

Living this way, no good for Him was I doing.
After the wrong things I kept pursuing.
But in His mercy He kept waiting on me.
So why did I wait so long and let this be?

Long ago to save me – He tried and tried.
Because living in sin, He was not satisfied.
Why did I waste all this time on me?
Why did I let this be?

Sin I finally realized was not God's way to go.
Christ tried hard the way to show.
I came to You with my head and heart bowed low.
The way to eternal life I now know.

Inspirational Poems of Encouragement

I WANT TO SHARE

The Good News with you I want to share.
When you are broken, God wants to repair.
And when there is despair and you are down;
Just remember God has His angels all around.

He knows what you are going through.
He has the right blessing just for you.
And just because the answer didn't come today,
Doesn't mean it isn't on the way.

Be patient and wait; He has a time and place,
All your problems with you He will face.
For me, for you, He suffered so much.
In your time of hurt He gives His special touch.

Never grow weary when no answer to prayer.
He hears your cry, he is aware.
Don't ever give up on the answer until He replies.
Wait and see what He gives, it could be a big surprise.

I waited and one day my breakthrough came,
And what a surprise I had. Things are not the same.
Now wait for your breakthrough, too.
Something good He has in store for you.

He always has something good for those who wait.
He will make your bad times good. He won't be late.
He knows all about your every need.
At the right time for your answer He will heed.

So wait and you will see;
Something good for you will happen as it did for me.
When you are down, God will lift you up.
You will rejoice when He fills your empty cup.

Inspirational Poems of Encouragement

OUR TROOPS, OUR VETERANS

Veterans, enjoy your one day in the spotlight.
When America called to defend her, you were ready to fight.
So remember, troops, we love you so;
For America, off to war you did go.

A medal of honor you might receive,
It isn't much for what you had to give.
We can never thank you for all you did,
And never know the fears you kept hid.

In fox holes or on dirty streets you might lie,
And for your country you might die.
You kept our Christian Heritage and America free,
For people just like me.

When you go to a foreign nation to fight,
You believe the cause is right.
Many fought and died for the cause;
Now receive our applause.

You fight a people you don't even know,
You are our hero.
You don't know when you leave if you will return;
For the family it is a real concern.

You never get the honor you deserve,
But this day for you we reserve.
For what you do, you deserve so much more;
You keep the enemy from American's shore.

Because of God and you America is still free.
Without you where would America be?
Today we salute those who lived and died,
We are proud of you; you did your job with pride.
"Thank you".

Inspirational Poems of Encouragement

THE EARLY YEARS

He left the splendor of Heaven to come to this earth.
We rejoice because of His birth.
He was born with the animals in a stable.
Without His death, salvation would not be available.

He was born in the little town of Bethlehem.
His beginning was not of this realm.
But there was a reason for Him to be born.
One day, He would talk about sowing wheat and corn.

There was a wicked king that wanted Him to die.
God didn't permit it, but he sure did try.
Wise men came and gave Him their wealth,
One day He would give people back their health.

But to Egypt with Joseph and Mary He did flee,
For His safety, there He must be.
It would be a long way back,
With only a donkey and a few things in a pack.

Did He have friends that with them He would play,
Or did He go and talk with God and pray?
Did He know one day from sin He would set me free?
Was He seeing things of God the way they would be?

In body He began to grow.
The things when He got older, did He know?
What were His thoughts at nine or ten?
Did He know one day His ministry would begin?

He must have learned much while He was young,
And many Jewish songs He must have sung.
"I must be about My Father's business," Jesus said.
The Scriptures concerning Him, He must have read.

At age twelve could He see on a cross He would die?
Could He see in someone else's tomb He would lie?
At age twelve could He see He would die for me?
Could He realize the agony He would suffer on that tree?

Inspirational Poems of Encouragement

THE LATTER YEARS

He is now thirty, His ministry would begin.
He would preach His message over and over again.
He would heal the sick, preach the gospel to the poor,
His mission in life has began, this we know for sure.

He was mighty in the word and deed,
And from little, the multitudes He did feed.
He came to seek and save those that were lost,
But to do so, it would be at a great cost.

Money from the mouth of a fish, His taxes were paid;
Life was found by the statements that He made.
He walked with God in faith and in power
He must do God's will, this was His hour.

All that came to him, He gladly met;
The woman at the well, eternal life she did get.
He lay sleeping in the ship, Him they awoke.
He calmed the mighty sea, by the words He spoke.

Jesus was always going about doing good,
But doubt kept Him from doing all He could.
But to others He said, "Thy faith has made you whole",
Then He was able to touch them, body and soul.

He marveled at their unbelief and doubt;
He would preach, "Repent" He would shout.
Signs, wonders, and miracles Jesus did.
The good news from the multitudes was not hid.

The hour has now come for Him to die.
The gospel He had preached; he did not lie.
The price was death. It has been paid.
The sacrifice for sin has been made.

His death is not the end of this story;
He has returned to all his power;
He has returned to all his former glory.

Inspirational Poems of Encouragement

YOU DID NOT COME

Lord, is serving You always like this?
It seems like I am already in the abyss.
I wish I knew if You were coming to help me.
My troubles overwhelm me, trouble is all I see.

There are troubles here and more troubles there.
It is getting more than I can bear.
I have always trusted in You.
Now I am at my wit's end, what am I to do?

I called and You did not come.
This race, Lord, is sure getting hard to run.
Never did I think this when I gave my life to You.
Now what am I supposed to do?

I just wonder, Lord, if You even care.
Your mercy You don't seem to want to share.
You left me with all this alone to bear.
And it sure has been a nightmare.

I called and You did not hear.
I came to You and You did not draw near.
I searched and You could not be found.
I reached out and You were not around.

When I sought You, You were not there
When I called, You were unaware.
When after You I did seek,
Not a word did I hear You speak.

You did not listen to me plead.
You did not come in my time of need.
After You I have always sought.
Has all this been for naught?

At the time of your lowest hour I knew.
At the time of your deepest despair, I knew that too.
And at your greatest pain I was there with you.
I have never been closer, I will see you through.

Inspirational Poems of Encouragement

JESUS, LORD OF ALL

Jesus, You are Lord of all.
I want to be listening to Your faintest call.
You will always be there if I slip or fall,
Jesus, You are Lord of all.

You created the worlds; they were created by You.
If I only knew all the suffering You went through,
So in truth and righteousness we must stand tall,
Jesus, You are Lord of all.

The gospel is sent that all might hear,
You do not want us to live in sin and in fear.
Because You want all to hear Your call,
Jesus, You are Lord of all.

Lord, You healed the sick and raised the dead,
And over the church You are the head.
Lord, You hear me when I call,
Jesus, You are Lord of all.

Oh that all would believe in Your Word,
It must be preached until all have heard,
And if everyone will heed their call,
One day it will be known, You are Lord of all.

Many say they know God but Jesus they teach not,
Give them a new heart, then for You cast their lot,
And preach the gospel and fulfill their call,
Then realize You are Lord of all.

I am going to do a quick work; and make it fast,
It will be quick, though it is still a great task,
And on each I will place a special call,
Yes, I am Lord of all.

Inspirational Poems of Encouragement

IN YOUR WORD I DELIGHT

When we are weak You make us strong,
You stand by us when everything goes wrong.
You touch us when we are sad,
You make us to rejoice, You make our hearts glad.

Lord, I have chosen the way of truth,
My walk with You started when but a youth.
Great and holy is Your name,
Never let me bring it to shame.

In Your Word I delight,
By it we put the devil to flight.
Nothing from You can we hide,
In You we are safe, in You we now confide.

My hands to You I now raise,
And my voice with thanksgiving praise.
Thy word have I hid in my heart,
And each day in Your Word I start.

Your Word tells me You are always just;
It is Your delight when in You we have our trust.
Thy Word is a light unto my path;
It shows me how to escape that day of wrath.

Forever in Heaven is settled Your word.
It was passed down until one day I heard.
It is a lamp unto my feet;
It will guide me until God's harvest I reap.

In Thy Word is still my hope.
And with it, all my troubles I can cope.
It shows me the way and what to do.
It keeps me until that day I go to be with You.

Inspirational Poems of Encouragement

MAKE MY HEART PURE

One thing I know for sure:
Nothing I did would make my heart pure.
You came to this earth and died;
I couldn't free myself of sin no matter how hard I tried.

If I was burned at the stake,
All it would do is my life it would take.
That still would not profit me,
Because in sin I would still be.

If I possessed all the world's wealth,
And enjoyed the very best of health,
It could not make my eternity sure,
Nor, make my heart pure.

If I could produce good works by the ton,
It would profit me nothing without God's Son.
If everyone's burdens I could endure,
It still would not make my heart pure.

If on a cross I would have died,
Still God would not be satisfied.
If I gave everything I have to help the poor,
It would not make my heart pure.

My righteousness Christ knew was a fake;
He still didn't write me off as a mistake.
His life He gave to make it sure,
So by His blood, my heart can be made pure.

Only Christ can change the life of a sinner,
Then in all things make you a winner.
This I have learned and know for sure,
Only Christ can cleanse and make my heart pure.

Inspirational Poems of Encouragement

www.ingramcontent.com/pod-product-compliance
Lightning Source LLC
Chambersburg PA
CBHW061645040426
42446CB00010B/1594